Learn to Play

Piano

in Six Weeks or Less

Learn to Play
Piano
in Six Weeks or Less

DAN DELANEY & BILL CHOTKOWSKI

STERLING

New York / London

www.sterlingpublishing.com

STERLING and the distinctive Sterling logo are registered trademarks of
Sterling Publishing Co., Inc.

Library of Congress Cataloging-in-Publication Data Available

22   24   26   28   30   29   27   25   23   21

Published by Sterling Publishing Co., Inc.
387 Park Avenue South, New York, NY 10016
© 2009 by Dan Delaney and Bill Chotkowski
Distributed in Canada by Sterling Publishing
c/o Canadian Manda Group, 165 Dufferin Street
Toronto, Ontario, Canada M6K 3H6
Distributed in the United Kingdom by GMC Distribution Services
Castle Place, 166 High Street, Lewes, East Sussex, England BN7 1XU
Distributed in Australia by Capricorn Link (Australia) Pty. Ltd.
P.O. Box 704, Windsor, NSW 2756, Australia

Sterling ISBN 978-1-4027-3156-3

For information about custom editions, special sales, premium and
corporate purchases, please contact Sterling Special Sales
Department at 800-805-5489 or specialsales@sterlingpublishing.com.

Contents

Preface by Bill Chotkowski

When creating a software package of piano lessons in 1995, I first met Dan and asked him to be the content expert. My company, Abaco, was developing software titles to be used at home on topics like piano, cooking, exercise, running and training, and career improvement. Little did I know that Dan and I would still be working together thirteen years later. We have become great friends and great collaborators. Along the way, we have introduced the piano to tens of thousands of people worldwide.

I've spent my career making computers useful to ordinary people. When I was a student at MIT, I was one of a handful of students looking at the usability of computers: how the "man or woman on the street" would use a computer. At the time, computers were expensive and unaffordable for personal use. Nearly everyone else at MIT used them to crunch numbers; decide how large to make a building's beams, determine whether a bridge would withstand wind loads, or discern the desired length of an airplane's wings. What interested me was how we could modify our technologies so that in the future using a personal computer would become as commonplace as reading this book.

Well, the future has arrived, and that original handful at MIT and I have contributed in positive ways to everyone's use of computers in various aspects of everyday life. Along the way, I learned to observe how people understood things and how to design software for novices as well as experts. I learned that I also needed to take into account how people understood the particular topic—whether it was cooking, exercise, or piano—presented in that computer software. I tried to design every button, prompt, menu, or graphic so that novices and experts alike could use it effortlessly. Naturally, this skill applied not only to interactive computer software, but to the topics as well.

This experience led me to write this book with Dan. The book is a blend of Dan's incredible piano and teaching talents and my talent for making complex topics accessible and understandable. First, we defined the book's goal. We wanted "a book that teaches students enough playing techniques so that they can take any lead sheet and play it, sounding great and having fun." Because Dan can continue to teach forever and has already written over 500 weeks of piano lessons—and he can describe another 500 weeks that he hasn't written yet—getting him to distill these into just six weeks took a lot of work. Refining those six weeks into the set of lessons that's needed to satisfy the goal of sounding great and having fun took still more work.

After we decided what we wanted to say, Dan designed all the lessons, created all the sheet music, and shot videos of himself teaching the lessons. Dan has a great multicamera video studio with specialized video switching gear that allows him to do his video shoots all by himself. You should see him with his hands on the piano, one foot on a piano pedal, and the other foot on specialized video switching gear. He controls all his cameras with his left foot as he plays the piano, and every video comes out looking like a finished performance that has gone through a video editing lab.

Using Dan's videos and sheet music, I created graphics to help illustrate the points he demonstrated on the piano. Then I incorporated all his instructions from the videos into the text of the book, adding the graphics. So even though I wrote most text found in these pages, the words originated in Dan's videos. We decided to present them informally as though Dan were sitting beside you at the keyboard, giving you the lesson. Constructing the lessons and format of this book have been a challenge for both of us.

We do feel that we have achieved our purpose. We have designed piano techniques that can be learned quickly and used by novices as well as intermediate players. These techniques are used by the pros—concert pianists. They will help you begin a lifetime of enjoyable piano playing, whether or not you ever take another lesson.

I hope you enjoy these six weeks. After the last page, at the end of the six weeks, I hope you will agree that this is the best book of piano lessons you've ever seen. Have fun!

Bill Chotkowski

Foreword by Dan Delaney

I began playing the piano as a young kid. I knew from a very early age that I wanted to become a professional pianist. Eager to pursue my dream, I enrolled in Berklee College of Music in Boston, just south of the city, while still attending high school. This initial exposure really prepared me for what was to come of my world of music. I also attended Berklee College of Music following high school, and I was able to network quickly, having been around the college during my high-school years, and soon opportunities began to unfold. At the age of sixteen, I began my private teaching practice and drove to students' homes, allowing fifteen minutes between the lessons.

Thirty years later, I still find myself teaching with a passion. I now have students of all levels: beginners to full-time performing professionals. I teach via the Internet with students in more than thirty countries worldwide, and I still work with select people in monthly correspondence. I'm a lecturer/author and provide an elite summer music camp for children. Oh, how things have changed! Through the years, experience has been my ticket to success and has put me on this path.

Following Berklee, I was eager to learn more and continued advanced studies under the well-known influences of Harvey Diamond and Charlie Banacos. In addition to my dedication to teaching, I love to perform. I play in all types of settings, from solo piano to trios and quartets, as well as accompanying singers. All are great experiences. I recall being one of the busiest working pianists in Boston in the early 1980s—always juggling both sides of the career: teaching and playing. As I sit back now and look at my piano playing and other professionals, I realize that I have developed a way to teach professional skills that can be communicated in an easy and accessible fashion.

This book is a result of all of my professional experience. I find that beginners can share many common techniques with professional pianists, and I have incorporated these into my method of teaching—professional skills used by beginners. This is the key to learning the fastest way of playing the piano. When students watch me play and I show them how I use these techniques, they clearly see the power of what I am giving to them. They see the skills I use as the foundation of my professional playing, and they cannot believe their eyes. They actually see it and hear it.

If you talk to people who have had piano lessons as children, you will find that the vast majority of them do not play anymore. They gave up at an early age because it wasn't fun (it didn't give them anything they wanted to do). Adults are the same way. Expressed in adult terms: If your efforts don't satisfy your goals, you won't make the effort. I assure you that this book will provide information that will enable you to play quickly by controlling the level of playing to keep it fun. You can present a challenge when and where you want and cut back your level in those situations that would normally frustrate you. In due time, you will welcome the challenge.

This brings us to the big question. Do you want to learn classical piano or do you want to learn to play using contemporary chord-playing techniques? I have found that the quickest, most enjoyable, most successful way to learn is with contemporary chord playing. I have nothing against classical piano; in fact, my skills will enable you to eventually move down that path if you wish to someday.

I know that chord techniques will enable you to work with simple options and grow from week to week as you learn new skills. So, actually, you have technique that is a faster way to learn piano and offers beyond what you could ever imagine. The illustrations clearly display the differences in classical music reading and contemporary chord reading. The classical template is done for you; however, each musical piece is written at a level that cannot be easily adjusted. Most often it is too difficult to play or, in some situations, too easy. With the chordal approach, a player at my level uses the same piece of music that a beginner would use. The method that I incorporate offers infinite options in my playing that enable me to control the chords and melody of the song. I will teach you, as a beginner, to explore those many options. It is an exciting feeling to actually have a student play a bar of music, and, when asked to do it again, have him be unable to recall what he did or which option he chose. This is what makes this form of playing exciting for me to teach. There is something within the music for all levels.

I will show you how to enjoy yourself and make nice music the first night, and show you how to build from there to a lifetime of enjoyment and improvement. Remember that the skills I teach are the same skills used by professional musicians. Those skills will grow as you spend time at the piano. It all starts here.

Dan Delaney

How to Use This Book

We have divided this book into 6 weeks of lessons, and, if you are dedicated, you can do each one in a week or less. We have even named them "Week 1" through "Week 6." Most of us, however, have other things to do and will spend a week or two on some of the more advanced lessons. You might even get distracted with playing your favorite tunes and forget to take a lesson for a week. You must remember as you get started that what I am about to present in this book will be well worth the wait. So be patient and do not rush through sections that you do not fully understand.

Each week has a number of lessons. The best way to attack them is to try to do all of the week's lessons every day you play, even if only for a few minutes each. The following weeks will present the same lessons at higher levels, and you will sound better day by day, week by week.

In every lesson, we include a description of what you are trying to do and how to do it. The lesson will be accompanied by sheet music and practice techniques to help you become comfortable with the skills of the lesson. The end of the lesson contains a review to let you know if you really get it. When you are comfortable with your review, you should move on to the next level.

Free audios of all lessons are on Dan Delaney's website: http://www.pianoinstruction.com. We highly recommend listening to them, because knowing how a lesson should sound makes it much easier to know when you are playing it correctly.

During the lessons, we point out areas where you can explore beyond this course, and reinforce it with a lot of enjoyable material in the addendum. If you find a place in the lessons that you really like, it probably has advanced techniques that you can explore in the Appendices. For example, we know that scales are important, but we don't think you really have to learn scales now. However, if you'd like, take a look at the scales in the Appendices. In truth, you don't have to do anything in the Appendices to enjoy the piano, but you could enjoy it even more if you knew everything in the Appendices.

Throughout the book, we show you how to use *shells* to quickly learn how to play all the chords in your favorite tunes. In separate exercises, we show you how to use *patterns* with a small number of chords in the left hand to provide rhythm and movement to your playing. By the end of the book, when you are comfortable with both shells and patterns, we will bring them together into a single, powerful technique that gives you the foundation for a lifetime of enjoyable piano playing. The inner parts of the chords (the 3rd and the 5th) are added to the shells and spread across both the left and right hands with patterns and movement that will bring a very professional quality to your playing.

Introduction

Throw away your *bass clef* and give your left hand a break—melodies in the right hand, chords and rhythms in the left hand. I'll give you a way to play many of the chords in the first evening. Certainly you will get more adept at playing them instantly in the weeks to come, but the first night, given a second or two, you will be able to play any piece just like the pros.

My system will focus on reading the *treble clef* in the right hand, while fully understanding the parts of chords in the left. If you want to learn the bass clef as applied in classical music, my method holds great value as a foundation for reading with your right hand, gaining valuable control before introducing the bass clef. But here is a word of caution about the bass clef: Bass clef pieces are written for a particular level of skill and must be played as written. An intermediate-level bass clef piece will be very difficult for a beginner, just as a beginner's-level piece will be too simplistic for an advanced player. With my chordal approach, a beginner and an advanced player can play the same piece. The beginner can play the piece with simple techniques, like playing only the root of the chord, while an advanced player can add advanced techniques to the same piece for a fuller sound.

Okay, your right hand is playing all those notes, what does your left hand do? Remember, the melody played in the right hand is always a high priority. Your left hand will support the melody, the high point of the music. My chord system enables you to quickly play all of the chords on the piano with your left hand. Whether it is maj7 or min7, dim7 or aug7, you will have the knowledge to play these quickly. Look at it like the foundation of a house. The professional skill taught here has you start by playing the outer edges of the chord. This is very easy to learn, and as you progress, you can enhance the musical picture by adding in the 5th or the 3rd of the chord. As easy as the chords are, always rest assured that this is a part of what professional players use in their everyday playing.

Although my chord method is a professional technique, you can begin playing right away. You start with one note, the root, and then move to the shell, ultimately filling in additional notes at your own pace. Each new idea creates an endless array of options to use as you play. You will always be adding to what you have already learned and organizing the groups of notes differently as you play.

Scales? They are important. Here's a secret: You don't need them now. Personally, I have spent years working on control exercises that have helped me greatly. However, not everyone out there is on such a focused path of piano mastery. I do recommend scale studies at the higher levels, but, at the beginning stages of playing, you should focus on learning to read the notes and applying chords. *Why do students practice scales?* They build strength and coordination. They help you to visualize the notes you use to fill in the chords and use in improvisation. All of this can be worked on after these beginning stages of development have taken shape. On the other hand, if a student enjoys applying the mechanics scales offer, they surely will not do harm, but rather offer the student more finger control on the piano. I have included instruction on scales in the Appendices for this book. They are optional. For now, let's get you playing the piano and learning that favorite tune.

The Appendices in this book contain lots of information that you should be aware of. I put these concepts in the Appendices because you don't need them to succeed with this book, but you may wish to start exploring these topics in the future.

Two, three, four notes in the right hand? You don't need them now. Concentrate first on playing the melody in the right hand—the single note. This is, in fact, the foundation for more complex applications. As you develop the ability to play melodies quickly and apply the shells of the chords, you will be looking for more to do. As your level gets higher, so do the number of notes you work with, creating more options for you to explore. You must understand that more is not necessarily better. The foundation you will gain from working with this book will have you sounding like a pro using just the melody and limited chord parts.

Counting: 16th notes, triplets, tied notes, etc. You don't need to learn them now. The important thing is to know your tune and play it at the pace you think it should be played. When you first start playing, how can you expect to count the melody of your favorite tune when you have all you can do to find the notes? It will become an important part of your studies down the road; however, you don't need to consume yourself with counting exercises at this time. I cover the basics of counting, enough to apply to the lessons to offer more of a challenge. In order to play now, focus on reading and chord structures. Choose to play tunes that you know, and everything will come easily. Eventually, when you get control of proper counting, you will open yourself up to a world of music out there and have even greater enjoyment.

Improvisation—it's easy. I will show you how. From the start, we will learn how improvisation relates to your options. Choosing one option over another is improvising. You are in control. My entry-level improvisation will have you sounding like you have been playing for years.

Fake books are wonderful for all pianists. Fake book music is most often associated with chord playing. You can never have too many fake books. You should go to your music store and find a fake book with some tunes you would like to play. Before you reach the end of this book, you can start playing from the fake book to give you even more interesting challenges. The fascinating thing regarding a fake book is that absolute beginners can use the same page of music as would the most accomplished professional pianist. You may hear people refer to *lead sheets*. They are just as the name says, the main sheet displaying chords and melody. A *fake book* is a book of lead sheets.

Each piece of music in a fake book will offer its own set of challenges. Often you will find chords without suffixes; for example, C instead of Cmaj7. I suggest you try 1-, 2-, or 3-notes-down shells to see if any of these are to your liking. Some situations have extra chords in a bar that are not necessary and can be removed to make it easier to play, and I will show you how to adapt to these situations.

Audio and video examples are available for these lessons. Often it is much easier to grasp a lesson if you hear or see me talk through it as I play. The audios are free as MP3 files from my Web site, http://www.pianoinstruction.com. I highly recommend listening to the lessons. The DVDs can be purchased from the Web site. Each lesson in this book will include the name of the audio to download; try one and you will find it enjoyable and informative.

Remember, it's easy and it's your music. This is what I tell everyone! If you can read the melody and play the *root* of the chord in the left hand, then you can play the piano. After all, this is the concept that I use when I play. Of course, I have played a lot, so I can easily use many more advanced techniques during my playing. I encourage you to begin with the melody in the right hand and the root in the left hand today. Enjoy the tune and the rest will come at your pace.

Okay, let's begin with Week 1.

Week 1

Reading: Where's Middle C and What about FACE?

Here's the first step along the way, and it's useful for both your left hand and right hand. The keyboard on a piano has 88 keys, some of them white and some of them black. Some electronic keyboards have 88 keys, and some have fewer, with the assumption that those real high keys and real low keys hardly ever get used anyway, so why pay for them. *You do not need to have a full 88-key piano.* You can learn how to play on scaled-down versions often seen as 61- or 76-key models. I do recommend that you have full-size keys on any instrument you decide to use. The keys should be touch-sensitive; that is, they get louder when you press harder and softer when you press more lightly. I also recommend that you add a sustain pedal to your keyboard.

When you look at your keyboard, you will see that there are a number of sets of two black keys as well as a number of sets of three black keys. These repeat themselves up and down the keyboard. Focus on the middle of the keyboard and find the two black keys. The note to the left of this pair is *middle C*. You should seat yourself at your piano with middle C in the middle of your body.

Throughout the keyboard, the note to the left of the two black keys is a C. Keep that in mind, because one of the things that makes this so simple, especially for your left hand to find chord letters, is that the position of a note keeps repeating itself throughout the keyboard, and there are only 7 white notes! The white key to the right of middle C is a D, directly between the two black keys. The D repeats itself up and down the keyboard as well, always between the two black keys. The next higher white key is E, followed by the white keys for F, G, A, and B. As you probably have figured out, these repeat themselves up and down the keyboard as well. Then we are back to C. Picture how each of these notes looks in relation to the nearby set of two or three

MIDDLE C

See how the Middle C is before the two black-note grouping.

Middle C
Found near the middle of the piano. Find the C that is just to the left of the center of your keyboard.

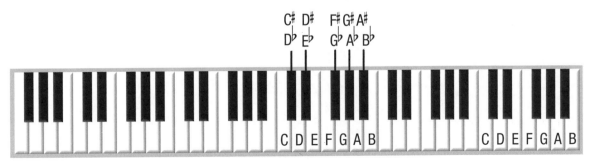

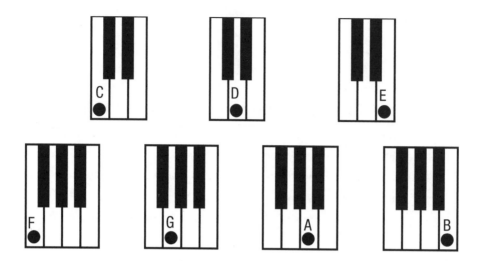

black keys. This is important, so I'll say it again, "Picture how each of these notes looks in relation to the nearby set of two or three black keys."

Play all of the C notes that you can find on the keyboard. Play with your right hand, and then play with your left hand. Do the same for the notes D, E, F, G, A, and B. Remember to picture how they look in relation to the black notes. You can use the images above to help you visualize the positioning.

Congratulations, now you know all of the white keys on the keyboard. *It's that easy.* You will learn about the black keys and sharps ♯ and flats ♭ in the third week, but just in case you run across some before then, here is a quick primer. A *sharp* ♯ is the next note higher on the keyboard, usually a black key, but not always. For example, C♯ is the black key just to the right of C. A *flat* ♭ is the next note lower. The keyboard chart on the previous page shows the position of the sharps and flats. That's it. Not all that difficult, is it? I will keep sharps and flats out of most of the exercises, until we cover them in depth in Week 3.

This lesson can be heard at http://www.pianoinstruction.com/intro.mp3.

What I Play, What I Don't

Below is an example of what classical piano music looks like. The top half of this is the *treble clef* where the melody is (your right hand plays this). The bottom half is the *bass clef* accompaniment where your left hand plays.

Wow! That's a lot to learn in 6 weeks, and it is very intimidating to the beginner.

But there is good news; you don't have to read music like this to sound good, play well, and have fun. Also, most of the professional piano players performing in the entertainment world use the chord method of playing, not the classical method of playing. As a chord player, I do not need the bass clef, although I have studied it and can use it when called upon. The chord system of playing will provide an easier approach to playing, and can be enhanced to very high levels in the months and years to come. If you are interested in the bass clef, I suggest you dabble with it later, and right now focus on my approach of chord playing for fast, exciting results. The chord system is in no way inferior or superior to that of bass/treble reading—they are just different styles of learning and playing. Remember that 99 percent of what I play is the chord/melody approach.

We can take that classical piece of music shown above and make it look like the example below. Now that's more like it. This is what I play. When viewing the sample in this form, you typically do not play the interpretation the same way twice and you will play it differently 6 months from now. In this book, you will learn multiple ways to play a tune like this, and this book will be the starting point for a lifetime of learning even more exciting ways to play tunes.

Music notated like this is known as a *lead sheet* or a *fake book*. You can find fake books in every music store, and you can find all of your favorite tunes written this way. You may even find books that also include the bass clef, and you can use them, but ignore the bass clef and use the chord symbols.

Treble Clef, Lines and Spaces, FACE, and EGBDF

The *treble clef* is where you play your right hand. The 5 lines and spaces that the notes sit on is called the *staff*. In addition to the lines and spaces, notes can sit on ledger lines above or below the lines and spaces. The treble clef can contain 3 octaves (or sets of 7 notes), which is a lot to learn without some help. That's where F A C E and E G B D F come to your assistance, and I will show you how they help in the first reading lesson.

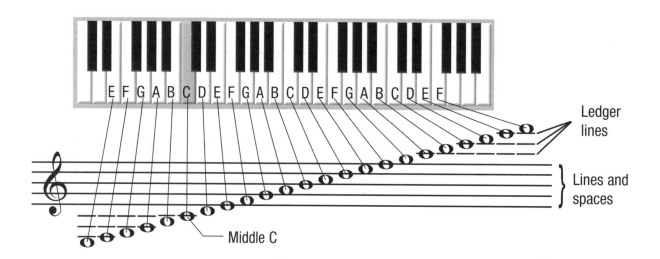

Your First Reading Lesson (No, not "Run, Dick, run.")

Begin with the "Treble Clef Lines and Spaces" illustrations on the next page, played in the right hand. To learn the treble clef, start with B, middle C, and D, 3 notes that sit just below the lines and spaces of the treble clef, with middle C sitting on a ledger line. Then learn the spaces of the treble clef where the notes FACE sit. The lines of the treble clef contain the notes EGBDF, remembered by the adage "Every Good Boy Does Fine." The rest of the notes shown in the picture above, those on ledger lines way above or way below the lines and spaces, can be learned later.

As quickly as possible, commit these notes to memory. If you have to recite through EGBDF every time to find a note, you will find yourself falling behind in your playing. Another way to quickly learn the lines is to remember the bottom line E is Easy, the middle line B is Between, and the top line F is Far.

Once you are comfortable with FACE, EGBDF, and the lines and spaces, you should move on to "Reading B through G" on page 6.

TREBLE CLEF
LINES AND SPACES

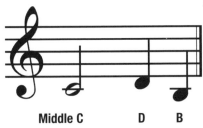

Middle C **D** **B**

These three important notes appear on ledger lines just below the lines and spaces.

Spaces

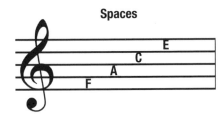

Spaces: Notice how the space lettering spells the word FACE.

Lines

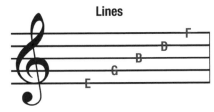

Lines: You must memorize this formula to achieve effective reading for the Right Hand.

This lesson can be heard at http://www.pianoinstruction.com/intro.mp3.

Reading B through G

Before you start, I want to explain what you are seeing in the music on the next page. Just above the music, you will see some instructions. You will find the instruction in classical pieces typically in Italian, and in some cases abbreviated Italian. Good luck! Fortunately, contemporary music has the instruction in English and it is mostly self-explanatory.

Reading left to right, you first see a 𝄞 that tells you this is the treble clef, or the G clef. That's the clef with middle C in it, the one that you will be playing with your right hand all the time. There are other clefs like the bass clef, but you won't see them in fake books and contemporary music, so they won't be covered here.

Next, you see a pair of 4s, which tells you that it is 𝄴 time, meaning that there are 4 beats to a measure and each quarter note gets 1 beat. Then you see some notes and rests on the lines and spaces and some chords written above the lines and spaces. The notes are what your right hand plays, and the chords are what your left hand plays. Some of the notes have a number above them, and these are fingering suggestions that I'll explain later.

There are some vertical bars in the piece that are called *bar lines*, and they separate the piece into *measures*; in this piece, there are 4 measures in each line (or system). There are numbers at the start of the 2nd, 3rd, and 4th lines. Those numbers indicate that the 2nd line starts with bar 5, and the 3rd line starts with bar or measure 9. Often an instructor or conductor will tell you, "Okay, let's start at bar 9 and see if we can get it right this time." You probably don't have to worry about that right now.

At this point, I want to give you a few words about counting. I have already mentioned the 𝄴 time, which explains the 4 beats to a measure. The notes and rests placed in each measure will always add up to 4 beats in 𝄴 time. Notes and rests (places where you don't play anything) have durations as shown below. For this reading lesson, all of the notes and rests are half notes and half rests, which means they receive 2 beats each. (You can take a look at Appendix C if you are interested in a more complete description of counting, but it's optional.)

𝅝 Whole Note (4 beats)	▬ Whole Rest (4 beats)
𝅗𝅥 Half Note (2 beats)	▬ Half Rest (2 beats)
𝅘𝅥 Quarter Note (1 beat)	𝄽 Quarter Rest (1 beat)
𝅘𝅥𝅮 Eighth Note (½ beat)	𝄾 Eighth Rest (½ beat)
𝅘𝅥𝅯 Sixteenth Note (¼ beat)	

Another little tip: Notes can appear like 𝅝 in addition to 𝅗𝅥; it's just a convenient way to keep those lines or stems out of the way of other things that might appear in the music. You will notice that notes on the bottom lines and spaces have their stems go up and those from the middle line to the top have their stems go down. Both of those notes, stem up or stem down, are still half notes receiving 2 beats. Also, a note followed by a dot gets lengthened by one-half of its value. For example, a dotted half note would receive 3 beats, not the usual 2, and a dotted quarter note would receive 1½ beats, not the usual 1.

Try this piece playing the root (or letter) of the chord in the left hand for 2 beats, followed by the note in the right hand for 2 beats. For the left hand, you can play the letters anywhere on the keyboard. For the slash chords C/E and G/B, play the letter following the slash, or E and B, respectively. Thus, for the first two measures, you should play

Beat 1	Beat 2	Beat 3	Beat 4	Beat 1	Beat 2	Beat 3	Beat 4
Left Hand: E		Right Hand: C		Left Hand: C		Right Hand: E	

READING B THROUGH G

Left Hand: Play letters of the chords.
C/E, play E; G/B, play B.

Count: 4 beats for each bar.
2 beats for left hand, and 2 beats for right hand.

Sight Reading: Neighboring Notes (2nd Intervals)

I find that *neighboring notes* are a very easy way to learn how to read quickly (sometimes without even knowing the note names). In this exercise, we look at the 2nd interval, which means the next note higher or lower on the lines and spaces.

Notice that there are a few fingering recommendations in the music, one at the beginning of each line. Your fingers are numbered from 1 to 5, with the thumb being 1 and the pinky being 5. The first recommendation is a 1 over the first note. That indicates that you should play this note with your thumb. Later on, you will find that you may want to put in fingering suggestions yourself on some of your favorite tunes. That's not cheating; that's being prepared.

Go through this "Neighboring Notes" lesson, playing a note higher or lower as indicated in the music. You will be astonished how quickly you can play this piece. It's easy. Try to not look at your hands—look at the music. Periodically, you can check to see if you are playing the correct note, but, as you get comfortable, you won't make any mistakes and you will have a great accelerator skill for your reading.

To help you keep your eyes on the music (and not on your hands), I recommend that you cut the side off of a shoebox, place it on the keyboard, and put your hands under it while playing. This hides your hands from your eyes so that you can't cheat and look at your hands.

In this lesson, each line can be played without moving the position of your hand. The fingering notated at the beginning of each line will correctly place your hand in a position that lets you play the entire line without repositioning your hand. In future "Neighboring Notes" lessons, you will learn how to move your hand smoothly up and down the keyboard as you play.

Once you are comfortable with the "Neighboring Notes," move on to the "3-Note Patterns" lesson.

This lesson can be heard at http://www.pianoinstruction.com/intro.mp3.

SIGHT READING: NEIGHBORING NOTES (2ND INTERVALS)
ONE HAND POSITION

Read the notes carefully, setting up your hand position. Try to play the line by feeling the intervals.

3-Note Chordal Patterns— Even More Fun for the Left Hand

Chordal patterns are a fun way to add life to your music as well as helping you keep time and follow a rhythm. In this lesson, we look at 3-note patterns for 4 chords: Cmaj7, Fmaj7, G/B, and Amin7. The patterns for these 4 chords fit nicely over the white keys of the piano. By the end of the book, you will be able to apply these patterns to all chords.

To play Cmaj7, play a C-G-C in the left hand, 1 beat for each note. You should play these with the pinky–index finger–thumb, or 5-2-1. Using the sustain pedal, press down with the first note of the pattern (holding it down for the entire measure) and then up and down with the start of the next pattern. On a piano, the *sustain pedal* is the pedal on the right. For most electronic keyboards, you can buy a sustain pedal to plug in to the keyboard, and I recommend that you do this. The sustain pedal will cause the whole pattern to ring. Also, if you have small hands, you can release the pinky in your left hand to reach the rest of the pattern and the sustain pedal will continue the tone. Another sustain pedal benefit is that it allows you to position your left hand for the next pattern while holding the sound of the current pattern.

The 4th beat of the measure is where the right hand plays. So, as you count 1-2-3-4, you play pinky–index–thumb, right hand. I have written this piece to have the left hand play followed by the right hand, allowing full focus on one hand at a time. You will also notice that I have indicated the notes of the patterns on the first line to get you started.

Keep the left hand near the right hand as you play. If the left hand gets too low, the sounds start to get muddy. You may even come across cases where the left hand crosses the right hand a little in the playing. That's okay.

These are the patterns used in this lesson.

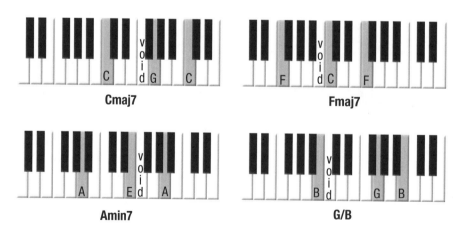

Get used to these patterns and then spend some time playing the tune on the "3-Note Chordal Pattern" music sheet.

Once you have mastered the music sheet, you can move on to improvising with these patterns. You improvise by playing any white note in the right hand along with the patterns. For now, you should play any white note, except for the void notes—there is one void note for each pattern. Later on, I will show you how you can use these void notes if they are quickly "resolved" to a neighboring white note, but for now stay away from them. You can even play pairs of white notes to add more color to your improvisation.

Appendix F gives you other patterns you can use for $\frac{4}{4}$ time, as well as patterns for other time signatures. I also provide suggestions for chord sequences that can be used while improvising.

The audio for this lesson can be found at http://www.pianoinstruction.com/patterns.mp3.

3-Note Chordal Patterns
(Cmaj7 = C G C) (Fmaj7 = F C F) (Amin7 = A E A) (G/B = B G B)

You must use correct fingering in the Left Hand. Pinky–index finger–thumb.

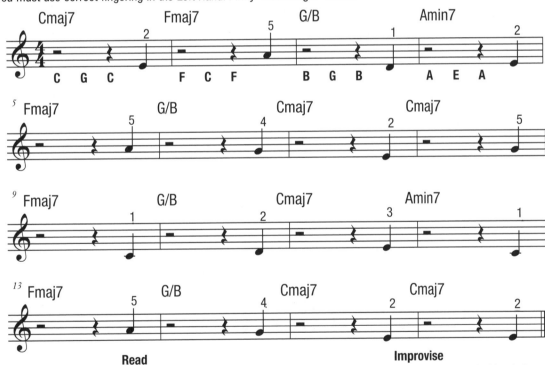

Read

Left Hand: Play the 3-note chordal pattern for beats 1, 2, and 3.

Right Hand: It is placed in on beat 4.

Void Notes

Do not play the F when using the C pattern.
Do not play the B when using the F pattern.
Do not play the F when using the A pattern.
Do not play the C when using the B pattern.

Improvise

Left Hand: Play the pattern while the Right Hand places in notes from the C scale (all white notes). One note is held for each bar.

Sustain Pedal: This device will help hold the sound of the chord while you are getting set up for the next chord.

Major 7 Shells

Shells introduce you to a very professional, very simple, very powerful technique that will be the foundation for much of your playing. In this lesson, you will learn about the major 7 shells. In the upcoming weeks, I will show you the shells for min7, min7♭5, dom7, aug7, maj6, min6, and dim7. They all will be as easy as these maj7 shells. In truth, once you understand the principle of the 1-note-down shells, the remaining shells will actually be easier than the major 7s.

Shells are created by playing scale degrees 1 and 7 or the root and the 7th of the major 7 chords. All professional players use them. In my technique, I will first show you the outer sections of the chords. The chords have inner pieces too, but we are only going to learn the outer portion of the chords in this lesson. In later lessons, I will show you how to add the inner pieces to both the right hand and the left hand. This spreads the chord across the piano for a richer sound.

By the end of the book, you will know how to fill in the shells with the 5th and possibly the 3rd, and merge the patterns learned in the previous lessons with the shells. These patterns and shells become one, along with 9 other options that will give you a multitude of professional techniques that you can apply to every chord in every situation you will ever see.

At this time, you may find that the 1-7 sounds a little dissonant or not pleasing. This is happening in these practice pieces where I have kept your right-hand melody separate from the left-hand chords. In future pieces, the melody will merge better with the chords to create a more tuneful sound. In later lessons, adding the 5th, as mentioned above, will change this dissonance into a full and beautiful sound.

Don't worry—it's easy and it's fun. But first, you need to take some steps to build a foundation.

You will see the major 7 chord presented in different ways by different publishers. Here are some examples:

major7   maj7   M7   Δ7

To construct the Cmaj7, find an octave in the left hand, C to C, with your pinky and your thumb. Then drop the thumb down 1 note to the B, and that's the shell for Cmaj7. It's that easy. For Fmaj7, find the octave F to F, and drop the thumb down 1 note to the E. For Gmaj7, find G to G, and drop the thumb down 1 note to the F♯. For Amaj7, it's A and G♯, and so on. Notice that sometimes the 1-note-down is a white note, and sometimes it is a black note.

Although you can play these

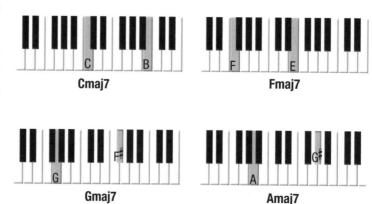

Cmaj7

Fmaj7

Gmaj7

Amaj7

anywhere, keep them higher on the keyboard, just below middle C. If played too low, your sound will become muddy.

For this example, you will be playing the left hand for 2 beats and the right hand for 2 beats. The sustain pedal plays an important part: Press down on the sustain pedal at the start of the measure, and up/down at the start of the next measure. This allows you to hold the sound while you are setting up for the next chord.

The audio for this lesson can be found at http://www.pianoinstruction.com/shell1.mp3.

MAJOR 7
(1,7 SHELL) C F G A
ONE-NOTE-DOWN FROM THE OCTAVE

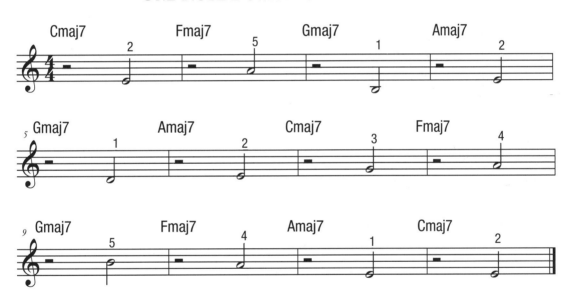

The major 7th shell is put together by using the root and the 7th note of the scale.

The shell can be easily found by having your hand placed at an octave, then dropping your thumb down 1 note. (Cmaj7 = C and B) (Fmaj7 = F and E) (Gmaj7 = G and F#) (Amaj7 = A and G#).

These are the various ways the major 7 chord will be displayed:
major7   maj7   M7   Δ7

Left Hand: Play the 1,7 on beat 1, and hold for the entire 4 beats in the bar.
Right Hand: Placed in and held for beats 3 and 4.

Sustain Pedal: This helps hold the sound of the chord while you are getting set up for the next chord.

Your First Tune: "Ode to Joy"

Although this looks complicated, with Cmaj7, Amin7, G7, etc., all you need to play is the root of the chord (the letter) in the left hand. For Cmaj7 play C, for Amin7 play A, and so on. For the slash chords G/B, C/E, and F/G, play the letter after the slash, which are B, E, and G, respectively.

Some suggested fingerings are included above some of the notes—remember your thumb is 1 and your pinky is 5. Try to keep your right hand in the same position as you play. You should be able to play the whole piece without moving your right hand, just choosing different fingers. You will notice that almost the entire melody is composed of neighboring notes, 2nd interval. Your exercises in this area will help greatly.

We won't bother much with counting on this tune; you probably know the rhythm, so play it the way it sounds good. Note that the low note at the end is an E.

To start, play one measure at a time and repeat it if necessary until you are comfortable. Hold the left-hand note down until you reach another left-hand note. Sometimes this is for the entire measure and sometimes for only half of the measure. At the same time, play the individual right-hand notes. Trying to get both hands working together is the most difficult part of this lesson. It is challenging at first, but soon you will be comfortable using both hands simultaneously.

Start stringing the measures together. If you have difficulties, you can try playing the right hand only and then add in the left hand.

Notice that the left-hand chords progress down the keyboard 1 note at a time. This little tip makes the piece much easier to play.

To make it a little more interesting, you can alternate the G chords in the 3rd line by playing one G, and the next G an octave lower, and back up again for the 3rd, and lower again for the 4th. This creates a nice sound. As you get comfortable, you may also want to try playing 2 notes in the left hand, an octave apart. This adds more depth.

This lesson can be heard at http://www.pianoinstruction.com/odetojoy.mp3.

"ODE TO JOY"

Week 1 Review

Let's review what you learned this week.

Reading

Can you find middle C on the keyboard?

Can you find all of the notes (C-D-E-F-G-A-B) on the keyboard?

Can you identify the treble clef?

Can you identify the lines and spaces?

Can you find FACE and EGBDF on the treble clef and on your keyboard?

Can you find the notes BCD that sit with ledger lines below the lines and spaces?

Can you identify how many beats are in a whole note, half note, or quarter note?

Can you comfortably play the 2-hand reading drill with your left hand?

Can you comfortably play the 2-hand reading drill with your right hand?

Can you comfortably play the 2-hand reading drill with both hands?

Can you identify which fingers the fingering numbers of 1, 2, 3, 4, and 5 apply to in the right hand?

Can you identify which fingers the fingering numbers of 1, 2, 3, 4, and 5 apply to in the left hand?

Reading Neighboring Notes

Can you comfortably play the "Neighboring Notes" exercise?

Can you play the neighboring notes without looking at the keyboard?

3-Note Patterns

Can you play the 3-note patterns for Cmaj7, Fmaj7, Amin7, and G/B?

Can you play the 3-note pattern tune?

Can you improvise with the 3-note patterns?

Shells

Can you play the major 7 shell (1-note-down) for Cmaj7, Fmaj7, Gmaj7, and Amaj7?

Can you play the major 7 piece?

Tune

Can you play "Ode to Joy" in the right hand?

Can you play the first measure of "Ode to Joy" with both hands? How about the first line? The whole piece?

TIP 1. ***Keep it fun.*** Always try to keep it fun. Music is a wonderful activity. Work within your ability and the time you have allowed for practice and have fun!

TIP 2. ***Establish small goals.*** Break each of your lessons into small levels. For example, play the right hand perfectly before adding the left hand, or, play the first 2 bars perfectly before adding the 3rd bar. This will give you multiple points of success within each lesson.

TIP 3. ***Understand why your material is being studied.*** I always explain why you are working on each technique and then I demonstrate it on the piano.

TIP 4. ***Small practice sessions.*** Sit at the piano for 5 to 10 minutes at a time—you will focus better and you will get more enjoyment from your practicing. So grab those 5 minutes before school or work and do this several times within your day while keeping track of it—watch your progress grow.

TIP 5. ***Don't rush to harder levels.*** Do not move ahead and be overly anxious to play more difficult material. It is everyone's tendency to want to go to that next level quickly. Be patient and the harder material will be easier if you take your time and learn the basics before moving on.

TIP 6. ***Use a timer.*** Back when I was practicing (as much as 8 hours a day), I had to manage my time carefully in order to cover the lesson material I was preparing for my teachers. By using a timer, you can allow 5 minutes on an exercise and once the timer goes off, you continue to the next topic. This will ensure that you complete all lesson material daily and don't overwork one particular area.

TIP 7. ***Stay motivated.*** Create a calendar and keep track of how much you practice daily. You can see clearly a steady pattern of practice and note those gaps on your calendar that may tell you why you are having trouble putting a piece of music together. Write down your times and pay special attention to those weeks when you have put in more time. Listen to the results!

TIP 8. ***Record yourself.*** Use a recorder to record yourself playing your various exercises and pieces, and then listen carefully to what you have done. Is it to your liking? Hearing yourself will quickly show you where you are succeeding and where you need to concentrate.

TIP 9. ***Use your ears.*** This will eventually be one of your most important tools for playing piano. Your ear will tell you a lot. So listen to it. If something sounds wrong, chances are it is, so check it out carefully and thank your ears for listening in.

TIP 10. ***Practice means playing what you don't know.*** Remember to get the most out of your time, and practice material that presents a challenge. When you sit at the piano and play without any mistakes, it is time to do something new and more difficult.

Week 2

Reading: EGBDF, FACE, and Full-Range Sight Reading

Last week we learned where to find EGBDF and FACE on the keyboard and on the lines and spaces in sheet music. This week the "Treble Clef (Lines)" and "Treble Clef (Spaces)" exercises give you an opportunity to focus on the lines and the spaces in your right hand while your left hand accompanies with chord roots.

Treble Clef (Lines)

On the "Treble Clef (Lines)" page (facing page 19), play the letter of the chord in your left hand, holding down for all 4 beats of the measure. Your right hand should add its note in for beats 3 and 4 of the measure. For the slash chords G/B, C/E, and G/F, use the letter following the slash: B, E, and F, respectively. Use the fingering indicated on the notes to keep the entire piece under one hand position.

This lesson and the following reading lessons for Week 2 can be heard
at http://www.pianoinstruction.com/reading2.mp3.

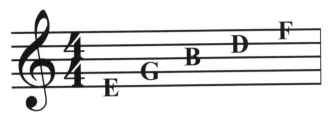

The following 4 lines of music will provide an exercise to enhance your reading of the 5 lines (EGBDF) in the treble clef.

Left Hand: Play the letter and hold for the 4 beats in the bar.

Right Hand: Read and play the lines of music in the treble clef. Keep under one hand position by using the fingering.

G/B use B; C/E use E; G/F use F.

Notice how your Left-Hand note is chosen from the right side of the slash.

TREBLE CLEF (LINES)

Treble Clef (Spaces)

On the "Treble Clef (Spaces)" page (facing page 21), play the letter of the chord in your left hand, holding down for all 4 beats of the measure. Your right hand should add its note on beats 3 and 4 of the measure. For the slash chord C/E, use the letter following the slash: E. Also, use the fingering indicated on the notes to keep the entire piece under one hand position.

This lesson and the other reading lessons for Week 2 can be heard at http://www.pianoinstruction.com/reading2.mp3.

The following 4 lines of music will provide an exercise to enhance your reading of the 4 spaces (FACE) of the treble clef.

Left Hand: Play the letter and hold for the 4 beats in the bar.

Right Hand: Read and play the spaces of music in the treble clef. Keep under one hand position, using the fingering.

C/E use E

Notice how your Left-Hand note is chosen from the right side of the slash.

TREBLE CLEF (SPACES)

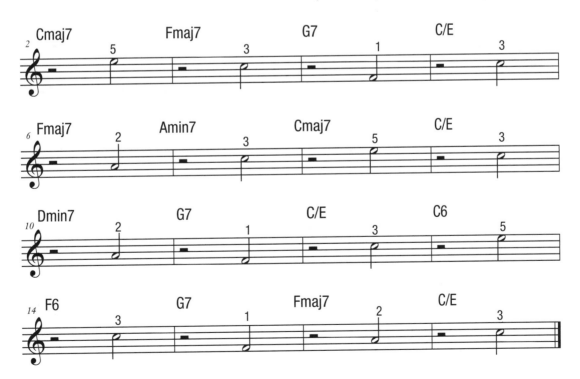

Sight Reading: Intervals, Full-Range Reading

In this section, I introduce you to repositioning your hand to reach the full range. You accomplish this repositioning by using the thumb as a pivoting point for switching your hand position. On the way up the keyboard, your thumb moves under your finger to the new hand position. On the way down the keyboard, your fingers move over your thumb. Don't worry—it's easy and natural, as you will see in the exercise.

Pay close attention to the fingering indicated above the notes.

Repositioning Moving Up the Keyboard: On the 1st line, in the 1st measure, the thumb goes under the fingers on the 4th note, effectively repositioning your hand 3 notes further up the keyboard. This happens again in the 3rd measure.

Repositioning Moving Down the Keyboard: On the 2nd line, in the 2nd measure, the fingers cross over the thumb on the 4th note. This happens again in the 2nd measure of the 3rd line.

Remember that it is always thumb-under or fingers-over. You will learn other repositioning techniques in future lessons, but for now we are concentrating on this crossover technique for the thumb and fingers.

Continue through the rest of the exercise, repeating until you are comfortable.

The Shoebox Trick: You can use a shoebox with one side cut off to cover your hands while you play. This should help you keep your eyes on the music and off your hands. It is important to get the feel of this and it is great practice. One of the common problems that beginners have is looking up at the music, down at their hands, and up at the music again. Then they have lost their place. This exercise helps you learn to keep your eyes on your music.

Advanced Technique: To build a better sound, add any white note in the left hand at the start of each bar. Most white notes will sound very nice, although a few will sound a little off. Pencil in those that you like. This will generate a nice sound and will also help you build your 2 hand techniques. You can even build up to 1 note in the left hand every other beat.

This lesson and the other Week 2 reading lessons can be heard at
http://www.pianoinstruction.com/reading2.mp3.

SIGHT READING NEIGHBORING NOTES (2ND INTERVALS)
FULL-RANGE READING

Read the notes, carefully setting up your hand position. Be very aware of the fingering notated to assist your hand-position setup.

Try to play the line by feeling the intervals.

3-Note Chordal Patterns: All-White-Key Patterns

This is a big step—getting all of the white-key 3-note patterns under your belt. You will master Cmaj7, Fmaj7, Amin7, G/B, Dmin7, C/E, and G7 in this lesson.

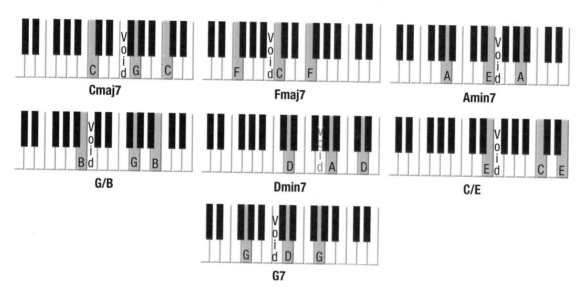

In this exercise, you should play the pattern in the left hand on beats 1, 2, and 3, followed by the right hand on beat 4. Remember to use the sustain pedal to help you out—up and down at the start of each measure. Sometimes, when you need to be challenged, you can change the right hand, playing on beat 1 rather than on beat 4. This is a little tougher, because the left and the right hands have to play at the same time. To make it even more challenging, you can play the right hand on beats 1 *and* 4.

After mastering the piece as written, you can try improvisation. First, you can read the left hand as written and choose any white note with the right hand. Then you can move to choosing anything you want for both the left hand and the right hand. To create nicer-sounding music, and to make it a little easier, stick to a few chords per piece. See Appendix F if you need help with making chord choices.

Remember the void notes that you should avoid until you learn about resolving them. When you get comfortable, you can add more complexity to the playing and depth to the sound by playing 2 notes at once in the right hand. Another idea is to play the right hand on beat 1, or beats 1 and 4. If you are really adventurous, you may want to try stringing a number of right-hand notes together.

Although these chordal patterns and the shells in the next exercise are presented as separate techniques, I will show you how to combine them all into one powerful skill by the end of the book. For now, use the patterns for improvising and the shells for playing tunes.

This lesson can be heard at http://www.pianoinstruction.com/patterns2.mp3.

3-NOTE CHORDAL PATTERNS
(Cmaj-C G C) (Fmaj7-F C F) (Amaj7-A E A) (G/B-B G E)
(Dmin7-D A D) (C/E-E C E) (G7-G D G)

You must use correct fingering in the Left Hand.
Pinky–index finger–thumb.

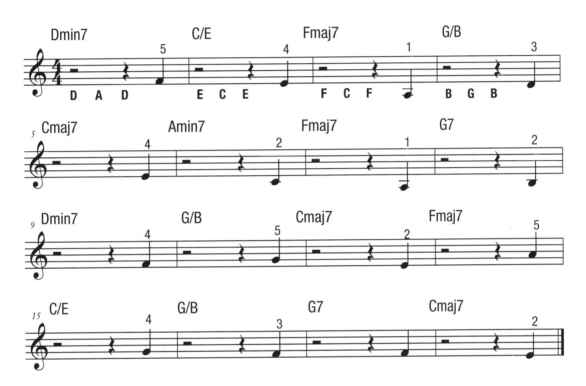

Read

Left Hand: Play the 3-note chordal pattern for beats 1, 2, and 3.

Right Hand: Play the written melody on beat 4, using the correct fingering. Thumb is 1; pinky is 5.

Improvise

Left Hand: Play the patterns while the Right Hand places in notes from the C scale (all white notes) on beat 4.

Major 7s: All White Keys

This lesson gets you playing the major 7s for all 7 white keys. These are easily found by placing your left hand, pinky and thumb (5-1), on the octave and moving the thumb down 1 note. Notice that 5 of the chords (Dmaj7, Emaj7, Gmaj7, Amaj7, and Bmaj7) have a black key at the top of the shell. These notes are sharps ♯.

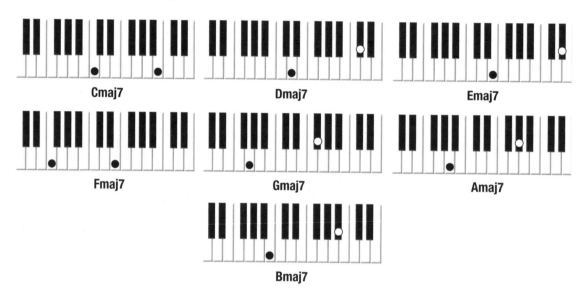

Sharps also appear in the right hand in this piece. In all cases, they are the black key just above and to the right of the white key of the note.

Go through all 7 chords in the left hand to become familiar with them.

To play the piece, hold the shell in the left hand for 4 beats, and add the right-hand notes on beats 3 and 4. Use the sustain pedal to help you hold the shell, and to make the measure ring. Pedal up and down at the start of each measure.

To play this piece smoothly, you need to be looking ahead to be prepared for the next measure. The sustain pedal gives you the opportunity to position your left hand for the upcoming measure while your right hand is playing beats 3 and 4. At beat 4, your left hand should be ready and positioned for the upcoming measure.

Your right hand will go up and down the keyboard as noted by the music. Where does your left hand play? It should follow your right hand up and down the keyboard. Closer is better because the music gets muddy if the separation is too large.

If the piece sounds too dissonant to you, move the 1st right-hand note in each bar to beat 1, and this will smooth out the sound.

This lesson can be heard at http://www.pianoinstruction.com/shells2.mp3.

Major 7

(1-7 Shell) White Keys

"1-note-down from octave"

The major 7th shell is put together by using the root and the 7th note of the scale.

It can be found easily by having your hand placed at an octave and then dropping your thumb down 1 note.

Cmaj7: C, B
Dmaj7: D, C#
Emaj7: E, D#
Fmaj7: F, E
Gmaj7: G, F#
Amaj7: A, G#
Bmaj7: B, A#

These are the various ways the major7 chord will be displayed.

major7   maj7   M7   Δ7

Left Hand: Play the 1, 7 on the half rest, and hold for the entire 4 beats in the bar.
Right Hand: Play quarter notes 1 beat each on beats 3 and 4, and be looking ahead.

Sustain Pedal: Helps hold the sound of the current chord while you are getting set up for the next chord.

"Danny Boy"

This is a traditional favorite.

In this melody, you will find many examples of neighboring notes; your exercises in this area will be very helpful.

Note that I have placed fingering suggestions on this piece that should work for you, but if you have small hands you may want to add some of your own.

As you start playing this tune, play just the letter or root of the chords in the left hand and focus on the melody in the right. If you are having difficulty, start with the right hand alone and then add in the left hand. After you are comfortable and need additional challenges, you can play either 3-note patterns in the left or the chordal shells. Find which works best for you. The 3-note patterns sound very nice, but they will test your ability to work with 2 hands at this point. Keep at it and you will be rewarded with some very pretty music.

Notice that in the 3rd measure, there is no chord symbol. In this case, repeat the chord from the measure before. This will occur periodically in this piece and in other pieces you play. You should always repeat the chord from the previous measure. The first measure has no chord symbol and it is a lead-in that should be played without a chord.

Counting is not too difficult in this piece. You already know how it should sound, so play it that way. Most of the notes are quarter notes, 1 beat each, with a scattering of 2-beat half notes, 3-beat dotted half notes, and 4-beat whole notes. Right near the end, you will see 2 eighth notes that get half a beat each; count "one-two and-three-four" and play on both the "2" and the "and."

When you try playing the 3-note patterns, you will notice that there are 3 chords that we haven't covered in the 3-note patterns: C, F, and G. You should play the patterns for Cmaj7, Fmaj7, and G7.

If you use shells and come across chords that you haven't seen yet, you will have to be a little creative here as well. For the C, F, and G, you can play just the root, or play 2 notes an octave apart (I call this an *octave*, and my co-author Bill calls this *no-notes-down*). Amin7 and Dmin7 can be played the same way for now, although they are really 2-notes-down, which we will learn next week.

This lesson can be heard at http://www.pianoinstruction.com/shells2.mp3.

"DANNY BOY"

Week 2 Review

Let's review what you learned this week.

Reading

Can you play the "Treble Clef (Lines)" reading piece?

Can you play the "Treble Clef (Spaces)" reading piece?

Interval Reading

Can you reposition moving up the keyboard by moving thumb under fingers?

Can you reposition moving down the keyboard by moving fingers over thumb?

Can you play the "Neighboring Notes (2nd Interval)" piece comfortably?

Patterns

Can you play all 7 white-key 3-note patterns?

Can you play the 3-note chordal pattern piece as written?

Can you play the 3-note chordal pattern piece improvising with the right hand?

Can you improvise 3-note patterns with both hands?

Can you improvise playing 2 notes at a time in the right hand?

Can you improvise playing right-hand notes at beats 1 and 4?

Shells

Can you play the major 7s for all 7 white keys?

Can you play the "Major 7" piece smoothly?

Can you use the sustain pedal to make the chords hold?

Tune

Can you play "Danny Boy" in the right hand only?

Can you play "Danny Boy" with both hands, playing the letters of the chords in the left hand?

Can you play the tune using chordal shells in the left hand?

Can you play the tune using 3-note patterns in the left hand?

Week 3

Sharps and Flats

It's time to move off the white keys and explore sharps and flats. What are sharps and flats? A *sharp* ♯ is the next note higher, and a *flat* ♭ is the next note lower. An example is shown below. Notice that a sharp or flat does not need to be a black key.

C sharp

C flat

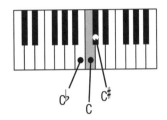

C♯ and D♭ are the same note. Also, D♯s and E♭ are the same note. This is called *enharmonic spelling*. Typically, every sharp is some other note's flat—that's the way it is.

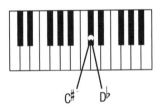

When a note is made sharp or flat, it remains sharp or flat for the entire measure. As an example, in the measure to the left, the first note is a C and the following 3 notes are C♯.

A *key signature* will appear at the beginning of a line, and it indicates that all occurrences of a given note(s) are sharp or flat. The key signature can be recognized as one or more sharps or flats written on the lines and spaces at the beginning of the line. In the line to the left, you see a key signature for the key of G, and it indicates that every F is an F♯, regardless of whether it is a high F on the top line, a low F on the first space, or any other F in the music.

Key Signature

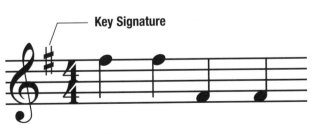

All 4 F notes are sharp.

F Natural

F Natural

Naturals ♮ will be used to cancel out sharps or flats. Naturals, like sharps and flats, remain in effect for the entire measure. Naturals work for sharps and flats indicated by a key signature, and for sharps and flats applied directly to notes. Both measures to the left are played F♯-F♯-F-F.

Treble Clef (Sharps and Flats)

Play the "Sharps and Flats" piece. Play the chord roots (the letter of the chord) in the left hand holding it for all 4 beats of the bar. Play the melody in the right hand, resting for the first 2 beats and then playing the notes on beats 3 and 4 of the measure.

Treble Clef (Lines and Spaces)

This is some more practice on the lines and spaces. Play the chord letters in the left hand, the melody in the right hand. In the left hand for C/E play E, and for G/B play B.

Additional Reading Exercises and Introduction to the Bass Clef

If you want to try more challenging reading exercises as well as get an introduction to reading the bass clef, take a look at Appendix I. This material isn't necessary to continue on with the book, but it offers an additional challenge if you want one. By practicing multiple notes in the right hand at one time, you will greatly improve your knowledge of the keyboard, and make most lead sheets easier to play.

TREBLE CLEF
(SHARPS AND FLATS)

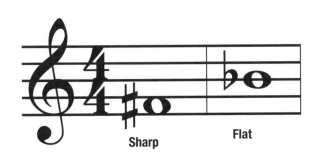

Sharp **Flat**

The following 4 lines of music will provide an exercise to enhance your reading of the 4 spaces and 5 lines of music in the treble clef, applying sharps and flats.

Left Hand: Play the letter and hold for the 4 beats in the bar.

Right Hand: Read and play the notes, trying your best to keep under one hand position as the notes move. Sharps move one half-step higher and flats move one half-step lower.

Sharps

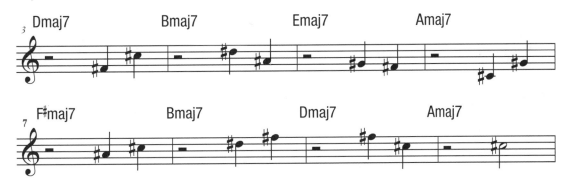

Flats

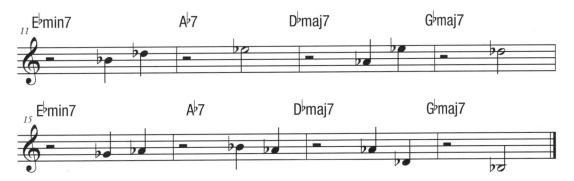

TREBLE CLEF
(LINES AND SPACES)

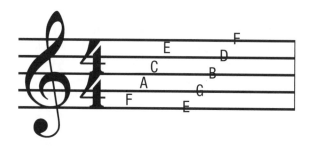

The following 4 lines of music will provide an exercise to enhance your reading of the 4 spaces and 5 lines of music in the treble clefs.

Left Hand: Play the letter of the chord and hold for the 4 beats in the bar.

Right Hand: Read and play the lines and spaces of music. Keep under 1 hand position by using the fingering provided.

C/E use E.   *G/B use B.*

Notice how your Left Hand is chosen from the right side of the slash.

2nd and 3rd Intervals: Under-Hand Position

Play this piece (page 36) without looking at your hand. In this exercise, you will be playing a neighboring note (up or down) or a skip (up or down), where you skip over the neighboring note.

Skips of the 3rd interval are always line-to-line or space-to-space. In this exercise, when you do a skip, you are skipping a finger to skip a note. As an example, at the beginning of this piece, you play the first note with your thumb (1), and you play the next note, a skip, with your middle finger (3), skipping your index finger (2). This keeps your hand in one place on the keyboard while you play the notes. In this piece, you will be able to play all the notes in a line without moving your hand.

Of course, not all melodies allow you to play without repositioning your hand. In the next exercise, you will start to learn how to reposition by moving your thumb under or your fingers over as you play in the next lesson. In future lessons, you will learn other skip and stretch techniques.

Make sure you start each line with the correct fingering, as indicated in the music. Try to get to where you don't make any mistakes, and when you reach that point, try using a metronome as an extra challenge.

SIGHT READING

(2ND AND 3RD INTERVALS)

UNDER-HAND POSITION

Read the notes carefully, setting up your hand position. Be very aware of the fingering to assist your hand position setup. Try to play the line by feeling the intervals of the 2nd and 3rd.

2nd and 3rd Intervals: Full-Range Reading

Play this exercise slowly. Pay attention to the fingering. This one is tricky because there are places where the thumb goes under the fingers on the way up the keyboard, or the fingers go over the thumb on the way down. It is always thumb-under or fingers-over, never the other way around. This will be obvious when you try it. Go slowly until you get it, and pay close attention to the fingering indicated at these crossover places.

When you are playing with fake books, you typically won't find fingering notated. You should work through the piece yourself and put in your own fingering notation to help you with the tune.

Read the notes carefully, setting up your hand position. Be very aware of the fingering to assist your hand position setup. Try to play the line by feeling the intervals of the 2nd and 3rd.

3-Note Chordal Patterns: Melodic Textures

This is a great lesson for both hands, and it is very musical. The 3-note patterns in the left hand help you to establish a time and a beat for your playing. This exercise also helps you to learn the notes.

Play these patterns using the pinky, index, finger and thumb (5-2-1), counting as you go. For the first measure, count 1-2-3-4 and play C-G-C-rest. The next measure is 1-2-3-4, B-G-B-rest. Use the sustain pedal to help you maintain your chordal tone. Pedal down at the beginning of the measure, as you play the first note of the 3-note pattern. Hold the pedal down until the end of the measure, and this will hold your chordal tone. Let the pedal up and then down again at the beginning of the next measure. This is a quick up-and-down motion at the beginning of the measure, going up as you are playing the chord at the start of the measure and right back down again.

This piece is designed so that you have time to look ahead for both the left hand and the right hand. For the left hand, the rest on the 4th beat, combined with the down pedal sustaining the tones, lets you look ahead and position your left hand for the next 3-note pattern. For the right hand, you aren't doing much while the pattern is playing, followed by a little flurry of activity, while the left hand is resting.

Remember to practice slowly; it will give you time to look ahead and plan your next moves.

If you need to see how the patterns look on the keyboard, take a look at Appendix F.

Eventually, you can add "colors" to the right hand. By colors, I mean adding in another note in the right hand—playing 2 notes at a time when you feel like it. Choose a white key to add in (they all will work, except the void notes), although you will find that some sound better to you than others.

When you are finished with the written music, try improvising. Play any of the patterns and choose any white note in the right hand, except a void note, to accompany the pattern. At first, follow the same rhythm that was used in the written pieces. When you are comfortable, you can try stepping out and creating your own rhythm in the right hand. This is a little more difficult, but you may find that you can slip in a measure or two of a different rhythm without many problems.

You can take a look at Appendix F to see more information on patterns.

Listen to this lesson at http://www.pianoinstruction.com/melodictextures.mp3.

3-Note Chordal Patterns

Melodic Textures

(Cmaj-C G C) (Fmaj7-F C F) (Amin7-A E A) (G/B-B G B)
(Dmin7-D A D) (C/E-E C E) (G7-G D G)

You must use correct fingering in the Left Hand. Pinky–index finger–thumb.

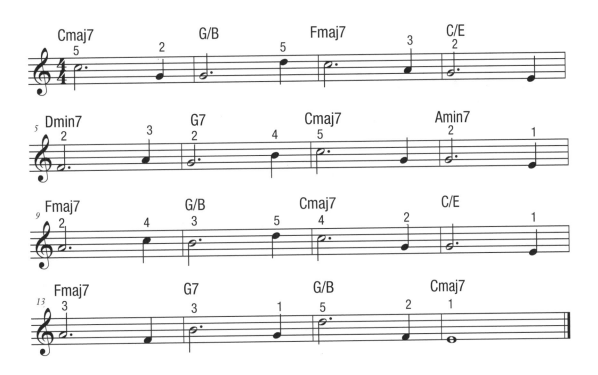

Read

Left Hand: Play the 3-note chordal pattern for beats 1, 2, and 3.

Right Hand: Play as written first; then apply melodic textures that have you place any white note under the melody, adding beautiful full sounds to your music. You may apply 2-note texture on 1 or both notes per bar.

Improvise

Right Hand: Play the piano using the white keys only and no music.

Left Hand: Play the patterns while the Right Hand places in notes from the C scale (all white notes), using the rhythm as above (dotted half note to quarter note).

Choose random 2-note textures in your improvisation. An effective way to start would be to have the dotted half rhythm play 2 notes followed by 1 note.

Major 7s One-Note-Down: All Black Keys

Now you are going to learn the major 7s 1-note-down for all of the black keys. You have already learned all the white keys. This exercise will complete the major 7 shells for all keys. Remember, you construct these by finding the octave and moving the thumb down 1 note.

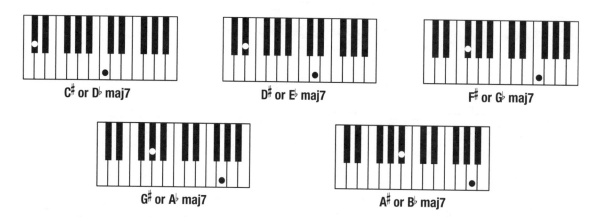

As you play the piece, remember to use the sustain pedal, up and down at the beginning of each measure. I've kept these exercises simple by having the left hand play and then the right hand, avoiding activity of both hands at the same time.

These major 7s may sound a bit cryptic or empty at times, but as you add in more parts of the chord into the right hand and left hand in the future, the sounds will smooth out. Remember that this is a very powerful and advanced technique used by professionals, so stick with it.

The audio for this lesson can be found at http://www.pianoinstruction.com/shells3.mp3.

MAJOR 7 C1–7 SHELL BLACK KEYS
"1-NOTE-DOWN FROM THE OCTAVE"

The major 7th shell is put together by using the root and the 7th note of the scale.

It can be found easily by having your hand placed at an *octave* and then dropping your thumb down 1 note.

B♭maj7 = B♭, A
E♭maj7 = E♭, D
A♭maj7 = A♭, G
D♭maj7 = D♭, C
G♭maj7 = G♭, F

Left Hand: Play the 1, 7 on the half rest and hold for the entire 4 beats in the bar.

Right Hand: Play the melody notes as written, using the fingering provided. Look ahead.

Sustain Pedal: This helps hold the sound of the chord while you are getting set up for the next chord.

"Greensleeves"

Let's look at the score for "Greensleeves" before we start playing (see page 44), and plan how we are going to play this piece.

First, we see that it is in $\frac{3}{4}$ time: 3 beats to a measure, and a quarter note (♩) gets 1 beat. That means we count 1, 2, 3 for each measure. This piece is a mixture of quarter and half notes, with 3 exceptions. At the end of the 5th line is a dotted half note that gets 2 + 1, or 3, beats. The last 2 measures of the second line and the last 2 measures of the last line contain dotted half notes tied together with a curved tie line. This means the 2 notes are played as 1 and that they get 3 + 3, or 6, beats.

Bar 7 contains a natural sign ♮ that cancels out the preceding flat ♭ for the D. Remember, when you see a sharp ♯ or flat ♭, it continues on that note for the rest of the measure. This happens for the C in measure 11; both C notes are sharp, even though only the first is indicated. A natural sign ♮ will be seen if the flat ♭ or sharp ♯ is supposed to end within the bar.

This piece contains an interesting road map indicated by the repeat signs and the ending signs. The repeat signs, which appear on lines 1 and 2, look like this:

When you come to the end repeat sign, go back to the start repeat sign and continue playing. The other road map signs in this piece are the ending signs, and they look like this:

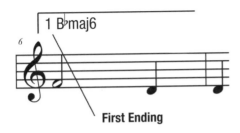

First Ending

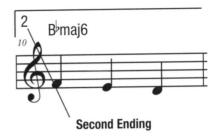

Second Ending

The 1st time through the piece, play the 1st ending.

The 2nd time through the piece, skip the 1st ending and play the 2nd ending.

So, following the signs in this piece, you should play:

The 1st line

The 2nd line (ending 1) and repeat to

The 1st line starting at the repeat sign

The 3rd line (ending 2; skipping ending 1 or the 2nd line)

The 4th line

The 5th line (ending 1) and repeat to

The 4th line

The 6th line (ending 2; skipping ending 1)

The chords in this piece contain some that you haven't learned yet, so just play the root (letter) of the chord for now. After Week 5, you can try this again using the 1-7 shells that you will have perfected by then.

Now that you have figured out how you want to play, start playing first with the right hand only, becoming comfortable with the melody. When you are ready, add in the left-hand chord roots.

The audio for this lesson can be found at http://www.pianoinstruction.com/greensleeves.mp3.

"Greensleeves"

Week 3 Review

Let's review what you learned this week.

Reading

Do you know what a sharp ♯ is?

Do you know what a flat ♭ is?

Do you know what a natural ♮ is?

Do you know what enharmonic spelling is?

Can you play the "Treble Clef (Sharps and Flats)" piece smoothly?

Can you play the "Treble Clef (Lines and Spaces)" piece smoothly?

Reading Intervals

Can you play the "Sight Reading, 2nd and 3rd Intervals" piece smoothly without looking?

Can you play it with a metronome?

Can you play the "Sight Reading, Full-Range Reading" piece smoothly?

3-Note Patterns

Do you know the correct fingering in the left hand for the patterns?

Can you play all 7 white-note patterns in your left hand?

Can you use the sustain pedal to hold the chord tone throughout the measure?

Can you play the right-hand melody along with the left-hand patterns?

Can you add in colors in the right hand?

Can you improvise your own tunes using the 3-note patterns?

Shells

Can you play all of the black key major 7s?

Can you play the "Major 7s (Black Key)" tune?

"Greensleeves"

Can you identify $\frac{3}{4}$ time?

Do you know how many beats to a measure in $\frac{3}{4}$ time?

Do you know what kind of note gets 1 beat in $\frac{3}{4}$ time?

Do you know what a natural sign ♮ is and what it does?

Do you know what repeat signs (‖: :‖) do?

Do you know how to use ending signs?

Can you play "Greensleeves" using the right hand only?

Can you play "Greensleeves" smoothly using both hands?

Week 4

Sight Reading: 4th Intervals

In this lesson, we begin by looking at the 4th intervals, which are much harder than the 2nd and 3rd intervals. You will have to look at your hand every once in a while to make sure you are doing okay. Remember that songs are written mostly with 2nd and 3rd intervals and a few 4th intervals, so when you have this down, you will be ready to glide through most melodies.

Notice that the 4th interval is a line to a space or a space to a line. Visualize this as you play. Go through the first page, which is mostly 4th intervals, checking your hands periodically to make sure that everything is okay.

When comfortable, move on to the "2nd, 3rd, and 4th Intervals" page. You should flow more smoothly through this page; the 2nd and 3rd intervals should go smoothly without looking. You will have to look at the piano on the 4th intervals to make sure you get them right.

Add in white notes with the left hand at the start of each bar. Pencil in the ones that sound good to you, just as you have done in the previous weeks. Maybe start by adding in the left hand on every other bar to make it easier.

You can listen to this lesson at http://www.pianoinstruction.com/reading4.mp3.

Sight Reading 4th Intervals Primary Focus

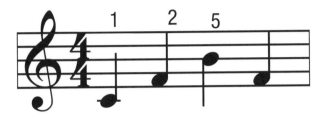

Note how the 4th skips from a line to a space or a space to a line.

This exercise will work on the 4th intervals. Be very careful, as this interval offers much greater challenge to feel the spacing as the notes move. Fingering will be notated to help position the line.

It is very important to move slowly through the lines below to offer yourself enough time to feel and see the 4th spacing.

Typical melodies will use a lot of 2nd and 3rd intervals. Be careful when reading 4th intervals and larger. Remember the 4th is line to space or space to line.

3-Note Pattern for Left Hand: 2 Notes Release to 1 (Options)

We are still working with all the white-key patterns, and this lesson introduces options for the 3-note patterns for the left hand: 1 using the 7th and 1 using the 10th, as shown below.

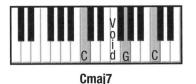
Cmaj7

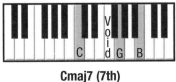
Cmaj7 (7th)

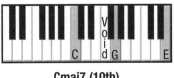
Cmaj7 (10th)

First, with your left hand, run through all 7 chords using the octave. Then try option 1, which uses the 7th. After playing with option 1 for a while, try using option 2, which uses the 10th. Remember that it is very difficult to become comfortable with all the options, but get started now and you will improve with time. The options are all based on the same rhythm in the left hand: 1-2-3-rest, 1-2-3-rest.

When you are comfortable with the options in the left hand, try improvising using 2-note textures followed by a single note in the right hand, and any of the 7 white-note patterns that you want in the left hand. Play the 2-note texture for the first 3 beats, followed by a single note on beat 4. A sample line is shown below so that you can see what I mean.

This is endless. Once you get the rhythm, you can go on forever. You can choose any of the white 3-note patterns in the left hand and play any white notes you want in the right hand. You will find that there is a void note for every chord that sounds a little "off," unless you resolve it quickly to another note. For now, don't play the void notes. You *will* hear them if you play them.

Play the octave as the pattern in the left hand for now. Move on to options 1 and 2 when you become very comfortable. See Appendix F if you need help finding the octave and/or 10th for all the chords.

You can listen to this lesson at http://www.pianoinstruction.com/patterns4.mp3.

Shells: 2-Note-Down

The chords min7, dom7, min7♭5, and aug7 are played using the 2-note-down shells. There are many different ways to write these chords; some are shown on the exercise sheet on the next page. Different publishers will use different written forms for the chords, so just be prepared.

Why can you use the same 2-note-down shell to play so many different chords? You can because the shells are the same for these chords; it's the inner notes that are different. That's what makes this so easy to learn. You are about to learn 4 x 12 or 48 chords in the next couple of minutes! Later on, you will learn how to play the inner notes in the right or left hand to add an even richer sound to your playing. From now on, you will use the shells to sound great, and in the future you can add in some of the inner tones to sound even better. I do this all the time in my playing. It's easy.

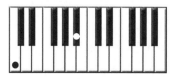

C min7, min7♭5, dom7, aug7

To build the 2-note-down shell, find the octave in your left hand and then move the thumb down 2 notes. Try it for a Cmin7, as shown to the left. You should find the octave C–C and move the thumb down 2 notes to the B♭.

Go through all the white notes and find the 2-note-down shell. Play them for a while, until you are comfortable with them and then jump around a little: Cmin7 to Gmin7 to Dmin7, etc. If you need to see what all the 2-note-down shells look like, please see Appendix A. After looking at it once, you won't need Appendix A at all; the 2-note-down approach will come naturally.

Try the "Tune Sample (Piece 2)." This tune is a mix of the 1-note-down and 2-note-down systems, with one exception. The exception is the Cmaj6 in the third line. For the Cmaj6, just play the root this week; in other words, just play C. This is a good example of what to do when you come across a chord you haven't mastered yet—just play the root. You will learn about the maj6, 3-note-down, in Week 5.

I use the 1-7 shells all the time in my playing. Keep at it and you will find them very useful as well.

You can listen to this lesson at http://www.pianoinstruction.com/shells4.mp3.

MIN7, MIN7♭5, DOM7, AND AUG7 (2-NOTE-DOWN)

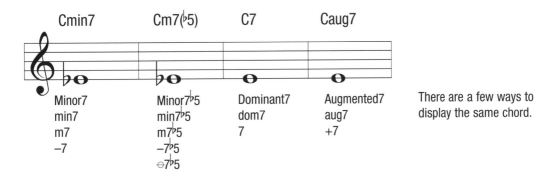

Cmin7	Cm7(♭5)	C7	Caug7
Minor7	Minor7♭5	Dominant7	Augmented7
min7	min7♭5	dom7	aug7
m7	m7♭5	7	+7
−7	−7♭5		
	⊖7♭5		

There are a few ways to display the same chord.

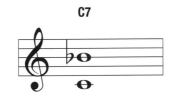

C7

The 2-note-down chord shell will cover the outer edges of the min7, min7♭5, dom7, and aug7 chords. Notice how the top note comes down 2 notes from the octave.

Tune Sample (Piece 2)

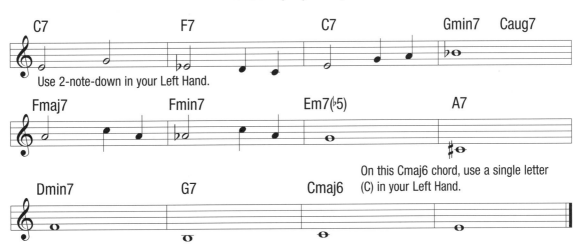

Use 2-note-down in your Left Hand.

On this Cmaj6 chord, use a single letter (C) in your Left Hand.

"Dixie"

A very nice tune with a melody that covers a wide range in the right hand. You should try to use the neighboring notes technique where it applies.

Start by playing the melody in the right hand and the chord roots (letters of the chord) in the left hand. Use the fingering suggested, although you can adjust it if needed to accommodate the size of your hands.

When you are comfortable with the tune and the roots, give it a try using shells.

There are a few places of importance that you should prepare for. First, in bars 4 and 5, play the F, using the 5th, which would be F-C followed by F-Cs for the Faug. F6 and C6 are 3-note-down, which we haven't covered, but you can figure them out from your understanding of 1-note-down and 2-note-down. The F6 is F-D and the C6 is C-A. Try these out a little before starting to play.

In bar 15, I like to add a F#dim7 as the second chord of the bar. You can write that in if you like. The dim7 is 3-note-down, so the F#dim7 is F#-D#.

When you're comfortable with the shells, you can try 3-note patterns. You need to do a little prep work before starting.

- Your 7 white-key patterns will work for all the chords shown; the important thing is to use the white-key pattern specified for the letter of the chord shown. In other words, there are a Cmaj7, C7, and C6 in the tune, and the pattern you know for C is Cmaj7. That will work for all 3 C chords. Likewise, for G you know G7, and that will also work for Gmin7.
- In the bars with 2 chords, each chord gets 2 beats. You should play only the 1st and 2nd note or the 1st and 3rd note of the pattern for each chord.
- In bars 4 and 5, play the same 2 notes for each chord that you played while playing shells.

Have fun with this one. The 3-note patterns with this piece will be the biggest challenge you have faced so far; there is a lot of movement in both hands. Once you get it, you will be rewarded with a beautiful sound.

You can hear this tune at http://www.pianoinstruction.com/dixie.mp3.

"DIXIE"

Week 4 Review

Let's review what you learned this week.

Reading Intervals

Can you identify the 2nd, 3rd, and 4th intervals?

Can you smoothly play the "Sight Reading (4th Intervals)" piece?

Can you smoothly play the "Sight Reading (2nd, 3rd, and 4th Intervals)" piece?

Patterns

Can you play 7 white chord patterns with the octave, option 1 the 7th, and option 2 the 10th?

Can you improvise using the 2-note texture dotted half notes followed by a quarter note?

Can you improvise using pattern option 1 or pattern option 2?

Shells (2-Note-Down)

Can you construct the 2-note-down shells?

Do you know what chords can be played using 2-note-down shells?

Can you play the shell tune smoothly?

Tune, "Dixie"

Can you play "Dixie" with the right hand only?

Can you play "Dixie" with chord roots in the left hand?

Can you play "Dixie" with shells in the left hand?

Can you play "Dixie" with 3-Note Patterns in the left hand?

Week 5

Patterns: 2-Note Texture and Quarter-Note Improvisation

In this lesson, you will concentrate on more movement in your right hand with 2-note textures and bars of quarter notes. You have already played patterns on the white keys using the octave as well as option 1 (the 7th) and option 2 (the 10th). Keep using these in the left hand, while in the right hand expand from the dotted half and quarter notes, sometimes putting in 4 quarter notes in a row. This is difficult because you will have to concentrate on both hands at the same time, but it is rewarding. A sample line is shown below.

Notice that I made this a little simpler by repeating the same chord on the left hand for 2 bars. This allows you to concentrate a little more on the right hand in the bar with all the movement.

If you have trouble playing the 4 single notes in the right hand along with the left-hand pattern, you can start by playing the right hand only and omitting the left-hand pattern for that bar. Later on, you can add in the left-hand pattern, as you become comfortable with the technique.

You can also try playing left-hand patterns only for a bar and then right-hand only for a bar. This allows you to concentrate on each hand until you are confident enough to play both hands together.

You will not have to be as aware of the void notes when playing the quarter notes, because the void note will always be resolved by the next note you play. When you become comfortable, you can start stringing together multiple bars of 4 quarter notes, and even throw in a couple of eights once in a while, always coming back to the dotted half as a resting point.

Remember to practice slowly and have fun. This begins to open up different kinds of right-hand movement accompanied by the left-hand pattern.

Patterns: Key-Note Release

In this lesson, I will show you the key note and key-note-release technique that will give more structure and a great sound to your improvisation. You don't have to use this all the time, but consider it a useful option.

In the illustration on the next page, notice that I have added a key note to the 3-Note Patterns. This key note is the 3rd of the chord, just as the void note is typically the 4th for all chords, except C/E and G/B. In those 2 chords, the 3rd is already in the chord, so we choose the 5th as the key note. Take a look at the drawing and notice how the key note is in the same position for each of the chords. This lesson will have you playing the 3rd in your right hand as your left hand incorporates the 1, 5, and 7. It is your first exposure to using all 4 parts of the chord structure and spreading the parts across both hands. At the beginning of the book, I let you know that we were going to do this, and here we are. You can learn more about using the 3rd in Appendix H, and you will want to continue using these techniques in the future as your playing grows.

In this exercise, you play a 3-note pattern in the left hand, just as we have been doing for the last 3 weeks. You can use the octave or option 1 or option 2. In the right hand, you will play a dotted half note (for 3 beats) and then a quarter note, leading to the next dotted half note and quarter note, just as we have been doing for the past few weeks.

The big step in this lesson is in the notes you choose to play. Start by selecting a chord to play in your left hand, and play the key note of that chord in the right. The key note will be held for the first 3 beats of the measure, and then you release to any white note for 1 beat followed by a note that is 1 note higher or lower to start the next measure. This will be the key note for your next chord, so choose your chord for that measure appropriately. You still have freedom of choice, but that freedom only comes in the choice of the quarter note and whether you move up or down 1 note from the quarter note. The left hand and the right hand are tightly coordinated at the start of each measure; the choice of a right-hand key note defines which 3-note pattern to play in the left.

The next page illustrates the technique. Note that in the first 3 beats of each bar, you play most, if not all, of the four parts of a chord, the 1, 5, 7 in the left, and the 3 in the right.

You can extend this to have a 2-note texture in the right hand at the start of each bar. Just make sure that the key note is 1 of the 2 notes that you choose. But remember, you don't have to use this technique all the time; you can throw in bars without key notes, or with multiple quarter notes as you see fit.

This is a fabulous exercise that is very melodic and pleasing to the ear, as well as an important step in understanding how to spread all parts of a chord across the piano. Enjoy it.

You can listen to this lesson at http://www.pianoinstruction.com/patternkeynote.mp3.

FINGERING OPTIONS 1-2 AND 1-3

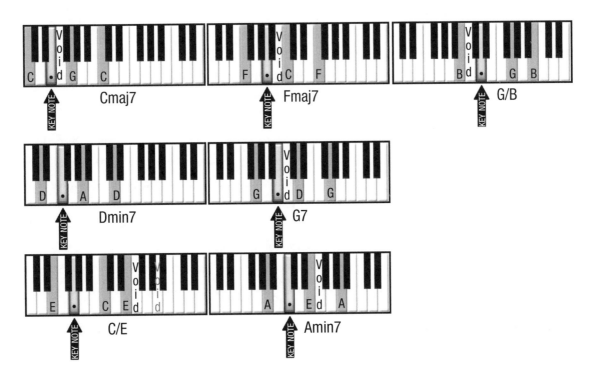

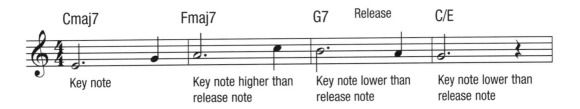

Cmaj7   Fmaj7   G7   Release   C/E

Key note   Key note higher than release note   Key note lower than release note   Key note lower than release note

Reverse Application of above 4 bars

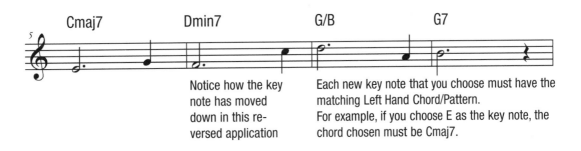

Cmaj7   Dmin7   G/B   G7

Notice how the key note has moved down in this reversed application

Each new key note that you choose must have the matching Left Hand Chord/Pattern.
For example, if you choose E as the key note, the chord chosen must be Cmaj7.

Fingering Options 1-2 and 1-3

In most cases, when you pick up your fake book, you will find that it doesn't have any fingering indications, so you'll have to figure it out yourself. You want to be able to smoothly move your right hand up and down the keyboard. There are no fixed rules, every hand is different, and every piece is different. You will find that 1-2 (thumb and index finger) and 1-3 (thumb and middle finger) are very important in generating movement over the keyboard. Play around with these techniques and find which ones are comfortable for you.

Play the ascending and descending lines on the following sheet using only the 1 and the 2. Always play 1-2, 1-2, but never, 1-2, 2-1. You will find that you can move your hand up and down the keyboard smoothly using the 1-2. Start each line with the 1, and when you are comfortable, repeat them, starting them with the 2. After you have mastered playing these lines with the 1 and the 2, try them with the 1 and the 3. See which is more comfortable for you, the 1-2 or the 1-3.

When you are comfortable with the ascending and descending lines, move on to the leap line. Notice that this line has a couple of leap points where the notes are far apart, in this case an octave for each "leap." Trying to use a 1-2 or 1-3 at these leaps would be very uncomfortable, so you must leap up with a 1-4 or 1-5 and leap down with a 5-1 or 4-1.

When doing leaps, the setup is very important. If you are leaping up the keyboard, it helps to set up to leap from the 1, landing on the 4 or 5. On the way down, it helps to set up to leap from the 4 or 5, landing on the 1. If your hands are large, you may be able to alter this a bit, but typically this leap setup is the most comfortable. Fingering is notated on the leap-line exercise. Try it to see how it feels.

Good luck with the pieces; they are difficult in places and when you make it through them all, you can take a deep breath and congratulate yourself.

There are no more note-reading exercises in the regular lessons of the book; however, if you want even further challenges with note reading, advanced note-reading sheets appear in Appendix I. You may not need them for anything you want to play right now, but reading practice always helps your playing, assisting you in finding the notes quickly and comfortably.

The audio for this lesson can be found at http://www.pianoinstruction.com/reading5.mp3.

FINGERING OPTIONS 1-2 AND 1-3

The power of the 1-2 and 1-3 movements is essential for best results in moving lines of music beyond the set hand positions. You will realize that there are many paths that feel natural; work them out and make note on your music for future viewing.

Different hand sizes will affect your options.

Remember: What is good for one hand is not always good for another.

Application 1
Apply 1-2 *(only)* on the ascending line and the descending line. This will provide focus on thumb under and second finger over for effective turning. Be sure to start both ways, with 1 and 2.

Also, reverse both applications.

Ascending Line

Application 2
Apply 1-3 *(only)* on the ascending and descending lines. Thumb under and third finger over will help improve your turning skills on the piano.

Application 3
Apply a mixture of 1, 2, 3 fingering on both ascending and descending lines.

Reverse both applications.

Descending Line

Notice how the *leaps* affect the turning function; more fingering options now become available—observe some effective examples written.

Interval Reading: 5th, 6th, 7th, and Octave

The 5th, 6th, 7th, and octave intervals are large or open intervals. These are the leaps that you practiced in the previous exercise. When playing these, you will have to look at the keyboard to ensure that you are getting the correct note. You will find that you often get back to a comfort zone following these leaps where the notes are close together and you can get back to doing your interval reading without looking at the keyboard. Go through the practice lines looking at the keyboard for the large intervals and then reverting to not looking in the comfort zone.

The 5th interval is a 2-line or 2-space distance. The 6th is outside 2 lines or 2 spaces; it's a line to a space, or a space to a line. The 7th is a 3-line distance or 3-space distance. The octave is outside the 3 lines or 3 spaces.

Good luck with the pieces; they are difficult in places and when you make it through them all, you can take a deep breath and congratulate yourself.

Shells: 3-Note-Down (Maj6, Min6, Dim7)

This lesson is the final 1-7 shell lesson. When completed, you will be able to use shells for any chord that you find in a fake book. You will have learned well over 100 chords! You will be ready to play anything.

To construct the 3-note-down maj6, take an octave and drop the thumb down 3 notes. As an example, for Cmaj6, find the octave C–C and drop the thumb down 3 notes to A. See the drawing to the right.

Cmaj6, min6, dim7

Try this with all the white-key chords until comfortable.

Try this with all the black-key chords until comfortable.

The tune has a mixture of 1-, 2-, and 3-notes-down. Play through the tune; play slowly at first to give yourself time to get the correct left-hand fingering. As you progress in the future, you will be putting additional notes in the right hand to add more color.

You can try tricks like pulsing the left hand, 4 beats per measure. This gives you another way to use the shells with a more up-tempo sound.

These shells will work everywhere, and they are the easiest way to learn the chords. Have fun—these will be a core element in your playing for years to come.

The audio for this lesson can be found at http://www.pianoinstruction.com/shells5.mp3.

SHELLS: 3-NOTE-DOWN

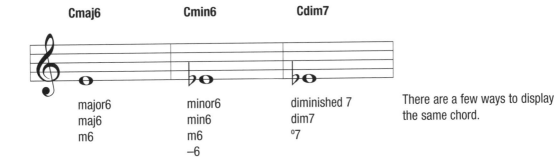

Cmaj6

major6
maj6
m6

Cmin6

minor6
min6
m6
−6

Cdim7

diminished 7
dim7
°7

There are a few ways to display the same chord.

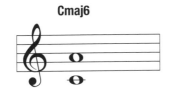

Cmaj6

The (3-note-down) chord shell will cover the outer edges of the min6, maj6, and diminished 7 chords. Notice how the top note comes down 3 notes from the octave.

Tune Sample (Piece 3)
Use 3-note-down in your Left Hand.

Blues Selections

Now you can have some real fun. I have written 4 blues tunes for you to play. These are fun, but a little tricky. Listen to the audio examples on the Internet to hear what they should sound like.

Pay close attention to the left-hand bass lines in these blues pieces. The left hand plays mostly single notes in these pieces; shells are used only where noted.

The left-hand bass line in "Funky Banana" is tricky: The 1st, 3rd, 5th, and 7th measures are played in the left hand only, and contain a nice little 4-note bass riff.

You can play these at your level now, and you can continue playing these, adding in new techniques as you learn them in the future.

The audio examples for these 4 tunes can be found at:
http://www.pianoinstruction.com/catmando.mp3
http://www.pianoinstruction.com/mabelsslide.mp3
http://www.pianoinstruction.com/funkybanana.mp3
http://www.pianoinstruction.com/buzzardblues.mp3

"Cat Man Do"

Dan Delaney

"Mabel's Slide"

Left-Hand plays root or shells where noted

Dan Delaney

"FUNKY BANANA"

Left-Hand plays letters as written
or root or shells as noted

Dan Delaney

Left-Hand plays root or shells as noted   "Buzzard Blues"   Dan Delaney

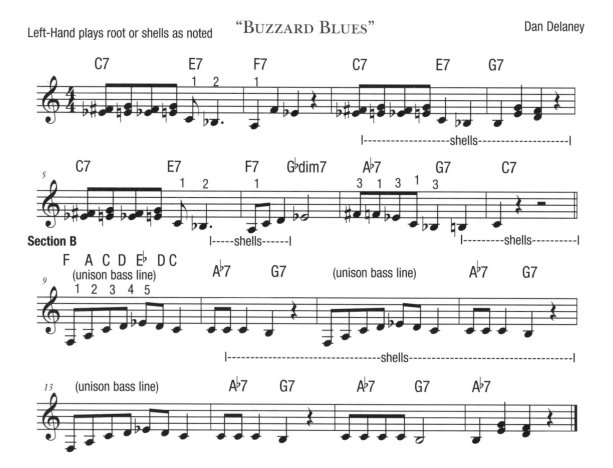

Section B

Week 5 Review

Let's review what you learned this week.

Reading

Can you move your right hand up and down the keyboard using the 1-2 and the 1-3?

Can you smoothly play the ascending and descending lines using the 1-2 and the 1-3?

Can you move your right hand up and down the keyboard using the 1-2 and the 1-3 with leaps included?

Can you smoothly play the line with leaps?

Can you identify 5th, 6th, 7th, and octave intervals?

Can you smoothly play the 5th, 6th, 7th, and octave interval reading piece?

Patterns

Can you improvise with 4 single notes in the right hand without the left-hand accompanying pattern?

Can you improvise with 4 single notes in the right hand with the left-hand accompanying pattern?

Can you improvise stringing together multiple measures of 4 single notes in the right hand?

Shells

Can you construct the 3-note-down shells?

Do you know the chords that are played with the 3-note-down shells?

Can you smoothly play the 3-note-down tune?

Can you smoothly play the 3-note-down tune with pulsing?

Week 6

Using 5ths to Bring It All Together

Throughout this book, I have told you that I will bring shells and 3-note patterns together at the end of the book. Now is the time, and you won't believe your ears. You are about to learn how to use the 5th to fill in the middle of the shells and make them into chords that are very versatile and offer many different options for your playing.

Finding the 5th

The illustration at right shows you how to find every 5th. It's easy. Take a look at C; the 5th and the root are five white keys apart. For C#, the 5th and the root are four black keys apart. This works for all notes . . . if the root is a white key, like a D, the 5th is a white key, and they are five white keys apart. If the root is a black key, the 5th is a black key, and they are four black keys apart. There is an exception, and that is B and B♭ (or A#). For those 2 notes, the 5th is a different color than the root, white root and black 5th, or black root and white 5th. Take a look at the B and B♭ to see what I mean.

Play through these 5ths. They are easy to find; they all feel like the same separation. After a few minutes, you should start finding the 5th almost instantly.

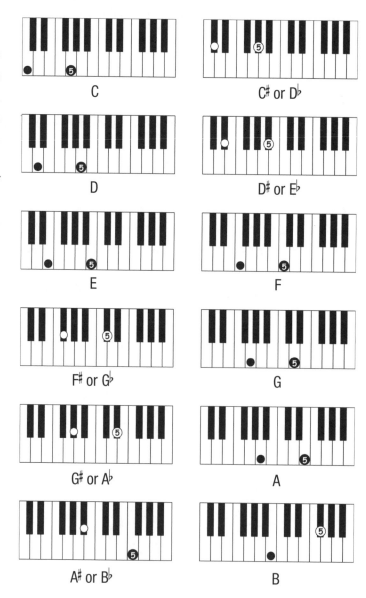

You can listen to this lesson at http://www.pianoinstruction.com/using5th.mp3.

5ths: The Bridge to Your Future

The following lesson sheet gives you 3 options to use while becoming comfortable with the 5ths. The first option has you play the shell, releasing to the 5th on the 3rd beat. The 2nd option has you use the 5th with the shell to create a 3-note pattern: 1-5-7. The 3rd option stretches out the 3-note pattern to be 1-7 high 5. The 3rd option will really stretch your left hand, as the high 5 is a little tough to reach. Use the pinky, index, finger, and thumb (5-2-1) for this pattern.

Play through the 3 lines using all 3 options. Options are very important, as you will see in the next lesson. When you are comfortable with this piece, move on to the next step to learn 10 options that you can use in your playing.

Remember that the 5ths for B and B♭ are the exception and go white key to black key or black key to white key.

Also notice that there are other exceptions that you may run across in the future. The following chords use altered 5ths: min7♭5 and dim7 use a ♭5, and aug7 uses a ♯5. Don't worry—just play the shell. Later when you are more comfortable, adjust the 5th to fit these chords.

1. Left Hand plays the 1,7 shell, and then releases to the 5th on beat 3. Use the (key) on the bottom of the page to help in finding the 5th.

2. Once you can play the shell releasing to the 5th, try converting to a 3-note pattern, playing 1, 5, 7.

3. Another good way to learn the 5th is to play a pattern extending in shape. Play the 1 followed by the 7, and then followed by the high 5th. (Use pinky, index finger, thumb.)

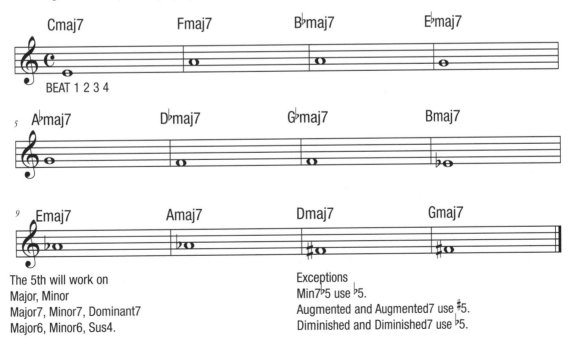

The 5th will work on
Major, Minor
Major7, Minor7, Dominant7
Major6, Minor6, Sus4.

Exceptions
Min7♭5 use ♭5.
Augmented and Augmented7 use ♯5.
Diminished and Diminished7 use ♭5.

Options Using the 5th

You are about to learn 10 options for playing chords, some of them using the 5ths. You will notice that some of the options are simple and require very little concentration on your left hand, while some options are difficult and require a lot of concentration on your left hand, especially when you are just beginning.

When do you use these options, and which one should you choose? You use them all the time, and you choose the one that will sound the best to you at the moment. Because you have so many options, you may never play a piece the same way twice.

At the beginning, you should choose a simple option when the right-hand melody is active, and then you can use a more complicated option when the right-hand melody is slow and easy. As you play more and more with these options, you will find it becomes easier to use any option at any time, but to start, pick your spots. Look for a measure with an easy right hand and use a complicated left-hand option. When the going gets tough for the right hand, choose an easy option for the left hand.

You can listen to this lesson at http://www.pianoinstruction.com/options.mp3.

The Held Options

Options 1, 2, and 3 are the shells that you have been working on throughout the book.

Option 1: Play the root of the shell, holding for the entire measure.

Option 2: Play the 1-7 shell, holding for the entire measure.

Option 3: Play the 1-5-7, holding for the entire measure.

The Broken Options

Options 4, 5, and 6 add some motion to the shells.

Option 4: Play the 1-7 shell broken 2 beats for the 1, followed by 2 beats for the 7.

Option 5: Play the 1-7 shell for 2 beats releasing to the 5th for 2 beats.

Option 6: Play the 1-5 for 2 beats releasing to the 7th for 2 beats.

The Pattern Options

Options 7, 8, 9, and 10 are all 3-note patterns built from the shells with the 5ths.

Option 7: Play the 3-note pattern: 1-5-octave.

Option 8: Play the 3-note pattern: 1-5-7.

Option 9: Play the 3-note pattern: 1-7-5.

Option 10: Play the 3-note pattern: 1-7–high 5.

Go through the lesson sheet, playing the first bar with option 1, the second bar with option 2, the 3rd bar with option 3, and so on. Notice how the bars with an active right hand use a simple option, while bars with a slow right hand use more difficult options. On the bottom of the sheet, notice the way to handle the exceptions for no suffix on the chord and for the C/E type chords.

When you are comfortable, play the following "Pattern/Shell Options—Application" to help you build a strong understanding of the shell formations and the 5ths in all keys.

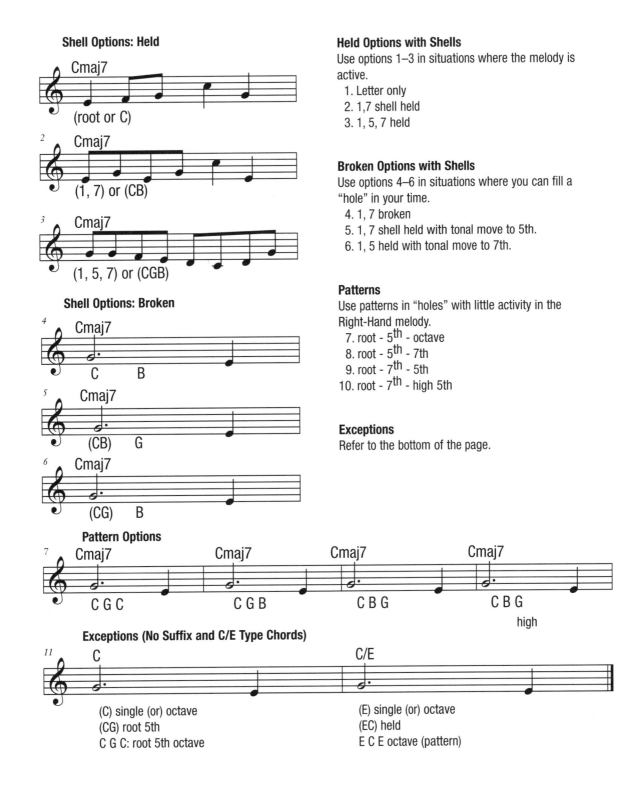

Shell Options: Held

Cmaj7

(root or C)

2 Cmaj7

(1, 7) or (CB)

3 Cmaj7

(1, 5, 7) or (CGB)

Shell Options: Broken

4 Cmaj7

C   B

5 Cmaj7

(CB)   G

6 Cmaj7

(CG)   B

Pattern Options

7 Cmaj7   Cmaj7   Cmaj7   Cmaj7

C G C   C G B   C B G   C B G
                                        high

Exceptions (No Suffix and C/E Type Chords)

11 C   C/E

(C) single (or) octave   (E) single (or) octave
(CG) root 5th   (EC) held
C G C: root 5th octave   E C E octave (pattern)

Held Options with Shells
Use options 1–3 in situations where the melody is active.
1. Letter only
2. 1,7 shell held
3. 1, 5, 7 held

Broken Options with Shells
Use options 4–6 in situations where you can fill a "hole" in your time.
4. 1, 7 broken
5. 1, 7 shell held with tonal move to 5th.
6. 1, 5 held with tonal move to 7th.

Patterns
Use patterns in "holes" with little activity in the Right-Hand melody.
7. root - 5th - octave
8. root - 5th - 7th
9. root - 7th - 5th
10. root - 7th - high 5th

Exceptions
Refer to the bottom of the page.

Apply the list of Shell and Pattern Options to this 2516 progression page.
A strong understanding of the 3 shell formations and the 5ths in all keys will be essential.

"In Walked Mo"

Left Hand plays shells

Dan Delaney

Audio found at http://www.pianoinstruction.com/inwalkedmo.mp3.

Placing the 5th

Now that you are comfortable with the 5ths, how do you place them into your music? You place them by looking for holes in the right-hand melodies. These holes may be rests, or whole notes, or half notes, or tied notes. The holes are any element in the melody where your right hand is inactive, giving you an opportunity to place the 5th in with your left hand. Examples can be seen in the first two lines of music on the next page.

What happens if you can't find any holes? In these cases, you can add the 5th in your left hand on the 3rd beat, even though your right hand is playing as well. This adds a nice steady bass rhythm to your piece. Of course, playing both hands at the same time is more difficult than finding holes, but it can be more pleasing to hear as well. It gets easier as time goes by. See line 3 for an example.

If all else fails, you can modify the melody a little to make space for the addition of the 5th in your left hand. Line 4 shows an example of modifying a quarter-note melody, holding some of the notes a little bit to make your own holes for the 5ths.

Placing the 5th

(X) Marks the Spot
(X) Marks the spot where the 5ths may be effectively placed into the music, lending itself to an interesting part in the music.

No Holes to Be Found
In situations where the holes are not clear, you can still place the 5th in on the 3rd beat, giving a nice steady bass rhythm.

Make Your Own Holes
The sample below (line 4 modified) illustrates how you can take a quarter-note melody and make your own holes.

Example with Holes

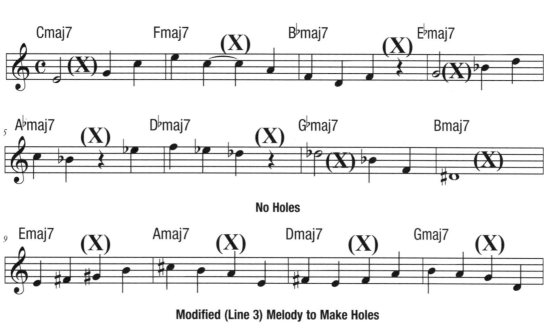

No Holes

Modified (Line 3) Melody to Make Holes
(X) Placed on beat

Putting It All Together
Add the 5ths and Maybe the 3rds

Fabulous, you have made it to the end, and you have the foundation to play any type of contemporary music. Adding the 5ths into the shells gives you a very professional technique that you can apply to all pieces. The shells and the patterns merge into one technique, a technique that can change in sound and complexity every time you play. You have options that will continue to grow with you for years to come. You now know so much that you may never play a piece the same way twice! If you want an even greater challenge, look at Appendix H to learn about the 3rd. Just like the 5th, the 3rd adds lots of depth to your playing and your options. You can add the 3rd in your left hand, or add it to the melody in your right hand. By adding the 3rd, you will be using all 4 parts of the chord structure: the 1, 3, 5, and 7. Usually the 5th is used as a timekeeper or as a way to give motion. Typically, it is added on a beat within a measure. The 3rd, on the other hand, is typically held throughout the chord.

Use the Left-Hand Options

When playing a piece and choosing your left-hand options, pay attention to the complexity of the melody in the right hand. Where the melody is complex with quarter notes, eighth notes, and lots of movement, choose an easy option for the left hand. Keep your eyes open for those places with whole notes, and half notes, and not much activity in the right hand. That's the place to add interest with some more complex left-hand options. Every piece will have a mixture of right-hand activity, some slow and some fast, and you can change your left-hand options as the right-hand activity changes. As you progress, you will find it easier and easier to place interesting left-hand options against any right-hand melody, but for now, look for the holes in the right-hand activity.

Fake Books

Go out and get some fake books, if you haven't already. Start playing and enjoying for the rest of your life. It's easy and it's fun.

Planning: Key Signature and Time Signature

When you choose a piece to play, you should spend a little time planning before you start playing. Look at the key signature and the time signature to know what notes may be sharp or flat, and to know your counting and tempo.

Know Your Chords

Take a look at the chords, and resolve any issue with the chords. At the start, there may be some you don't know. I have given you a number of options for resolving those, starting with playing just the root. Also, decide where you must play easy options with your left hand and where you can try options with more complexity.

Plan Your Fingering

Take a look at the melody and plan your fingering. It may be notated for you, or you may need to figure it out yourself. If necessary, pencil in your fingering notes.

Observe All Road Maps and Signposts

Look at the signposts of the piece, the repeats, the endings (the codas), and determine how you are going to play through it. Refer to Appendix G.

Mark Up Your Piece

Don't be afraid to use a pencil to write notes on your pieces. Everybody does it. I was at the opera last summer and saw the lead violinist marking up her solo during intermission while the rest of the orchestra was off having some refreshments. Here was a professional, at the top of her game, playing a piece that she certainly had played before, and she still was making notes to be prepared to play at her best. And, by the way, she was great when her time came in the second act.

Right Hand, Then Left Hand

Start playing a piece by going through with the right hand only, and then you can start adding in the left hand. Sometimes you may need to play a bar or 2 at a time until you are comfortable. Keep working until it all comes together.

Start Using a Metronome

You can give your playing consistency by using a metronome to help you with your counting and your pace. Be sure you can count out loud as you play before you start using a metronome. Set the speed of the metronome to what feels comfortable, using one click of the metronome as 1 beat in your playing. If you need to feel challenged, increase the speed a bit.

Listen to this lesson at http://www.pianoinstruction.com/together.mp3.

What's in the Future?

Now that you have completed the most effective foundation system for chord playing, you have options as to what lies ahead. You now have a great foundation for classical piano, and you can enjoy chord playing while you find some lessons for traditional playing. Or, you can continue on the path of contemporary playing. What lies ahead on that path will only enhance the great sounds you are already playing. Here is some insight into how you can build on this solid foundation.

You Know Chords and How to Use Them

Chords are made up of chord tones. You are now familiar with the root, 5th, and 7th for all of the chords. This is a powerful source to be used with the melodies that are found in everyday playing. You can enjoy your playing using what you know now, but there is more. The next additions to the system can be very exciting and can complete the chord-building process.

3rds and ♭3rds

The 3rd or ♭3rd will establish the major or minor tonality of a chord and will enhance the melody, shell, and 5th beautifully. I work the 3rd of the chord into the right hand, and this spreads the chord parts between two hands over the piano. If you visualize a melody, you would place the 3rd or the ♭3rd below the melody in the right hand, depending on the chord. The left-hand function remains the same as presented in this book using the 1-7-5 shell and the pattern options.

You can learn to deliver the 3rd in other ways. You can insert it in the left hand as the chord is played, you can use it as an *inner tonal movement* similar to the placing of the 5th in some of the options you have already learned, or you can place the 3rd into the right hand, enhancing the placement of that sound. These are just more options to add to those you already have.

Unlike traditional chord instruction where you pick out a memorized chord form in the left hand, my system uses a *broken application*, where you view the chord between two hands, inserting the specific degrees in a controlled manner. Traditional chord methods have you playing the 4 chord parts under 1 hand position. This tends to have people playing the chords by memorization, not by really knowing the chord parts. My system has proven to be far more effective in learning the chord parts, tone by tone, and ultimately providing you with a real professional application of 2-handed chord playing at the same time. My inner tonal movement concept is a true professional skill that enhances chord part learning while giving you the beautiful interest of the sounds dropping in where you want them.

Tensions: the 9th, 11th, 13th, ♯11th, etc.

Non-chord tones are referred to as *tensions* and can add depth to my initial system of chord building. Each new component of the chord—for example, the 9th, 11th, 13th, ♯11th, etc.—can be placed in as an added element within your playing. I know these are very intimidating to most of us, but I can assure you that with my organized approach, you will be playing the 9th as easily as the root. As you learn the more advanced chordal parts, the underlying chord tones become even stronger and more accessible.

I have spent more than 30 years organizing this approach and using it myself, and I feel there is no better way to achieve professional chordal sounds. This system is what every true professional chord-playing musician uses. In fact, when many chord-playing students come to study with me, they find out that they really don't have an organized approach and, subsequently, they have no freedom when they play a piece. Most often, they are doubling tones that are not necessary and would be better directed to have each finger using a specific task.

More Than Just Chords

There is so much more to playing piano than just playing beautiful chords.

Improvisation

There is *improvisation* that is developed from the knowledge of chord tones. Improvisation can also be pulled into music from the knowledge of scales. Improvisation is an extension of playing that can be brought in at the early stages. It can be as simple as delaying a melody to insert a personal touch. It is rewarding and helps to generate a style that is uniquely your own.

Reharmonization

Adjusting the chords that are written in fake book sheets is a wonderful level to achieve in your playing. Many chords can be replaced with alternatives adding a new sound, or the chords can be approached with others. An effective favorite of mine is to chromatically approach chords using a dominant seventh chord. Essentially, you are placing in additional chords that will lead into the existing ones.

Technique

Technique becomes a strong focus at the intermediate levels of playing. As you progress, you will want to explore a variety of tempos and alternatives. Your hands must be able to effectively control the notes on the piano to achieve these goals. Through musical exercises, you can achieve speed and control of your melodies and ideas on the instrument. Just playing is not enough—you must continue learning as well. You have played exercises throughout this book because they are the most efficient means to developing the techniques that you need. In the future, you should look for additional techniques that you can practice until you are comfortable enough to use them in your playing.

Listen to this lesson at http://www.pianoinstruction.com/more.mp3.

In Closing

I can go on and on about the many things on the piano that can benefit each and every person. Each student is an individual with a unique set of goals. My best advice to you when you play daily is to remember to practice things you cannot do. It is up to you or your teacher to present the challenge that is best for you. Most piano students say they practice every day but they are playing the same old tune—sounding great but not moving forward. I divide my time carefully for my students.

Practice time: Play what you don't know.

Play time: Play anything as often as you like.

The practice time is the essential element needed to achieve the most success on the instrument.

I hope this brief insight as to what is to come excites you to keep moving forward. Each new skill you learn will bring back great joy on the piano.

As a closing remark, you must remember that even as professionals at the highest level of playing, we use what I have taught you in this book. As you master the new skills to come, you can always adjust your playing options to reach within your means, meeting the challenge you wish to face.

Most of all, have fun. I hope you have enjoyed learning my method and my secrets. I certainly have enjoyed bringing them to you. Use them in your playing and you can look forward to many years of enjoyable music.

Dan Delaney

P.S. Look for my follow-up books where I expand on the techniques learned here to take you to greater levels of playing and enjoyment.

Listen to this lesson at http://www.pianoinstruction.com/closing.mp3.

Appendices

Appendix A: 1-7 Shells

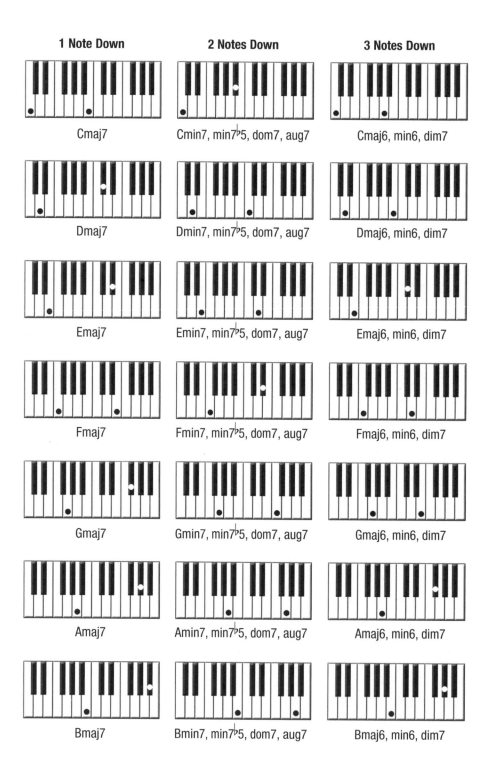

1 Note Down	2 Notes Down	3 Notes Down
Cmaj7	Cmin7, min7♭5, dom7, aug7	Cmaj6, min6, dim7
Dmaj7	Dmin7, min7♭5, dom7, aug7	Dmaj6, min6, dim7
Emaj7	Emin7, min7♭5, dom7, aug7	Emaj6, min6, dim7
Fmaj7	Fmin7, min7♭5, dom7, aug7	Fmaj6, min6, dim7
Gmaj7	Gmin7, min7♭5, dom7, aug7	Gmaj6, min6, dim7
Amaj7	Amin7, min7♭5, dom7, aug7	Amaj6, min6, dim7
Bmaj7	Bmin7, min7♭5, dom7, aug7	Bmaj6, min6, dim7

1 Note Down

D♭ or C♯ maj7

E♭ or D♯ maj7

G♭ or F♯ maj7

A♭ or G♯ maj7

B♭ or A♯ maj7

2 Notes Down

D♭ or C♯ min7, min7♭5, dom7, aug7

E♭ or D♯ min7, min7♭5, dom7, aug7

G♭ or F♯ min7, min7♭5, dom7, aug7

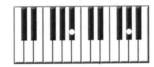

A♭ or G♯ min7, min7♭5, dom7, aug7

B♭ or A♯ min7, min7♭5, dom7, aug7

3 Notes Down

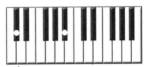

D♭ or C♯ maj6, min6, dim7

E♭ or D♯ maj6, min6, dim7

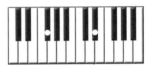

G♭ or F♯ maj6, min6, dim7

A♭ or G♯ maj6, min6, dim7

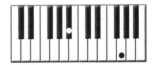

B♭ or A♯ maj6, min6, dim7

Appendix B: All Chords

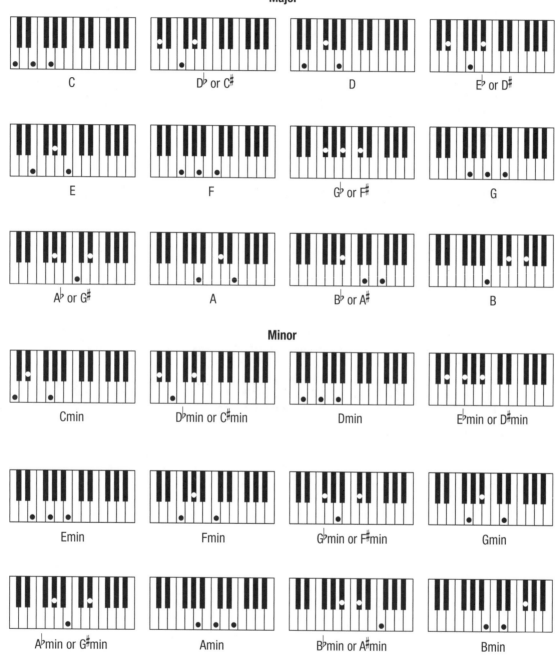

Diminished

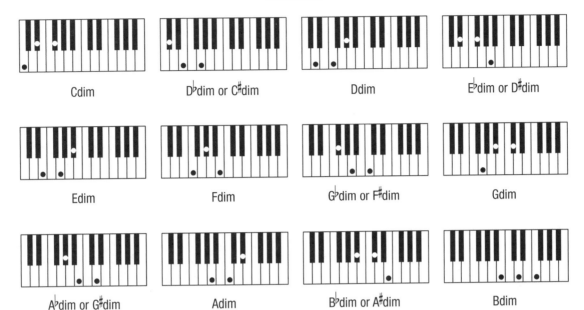

Augmented

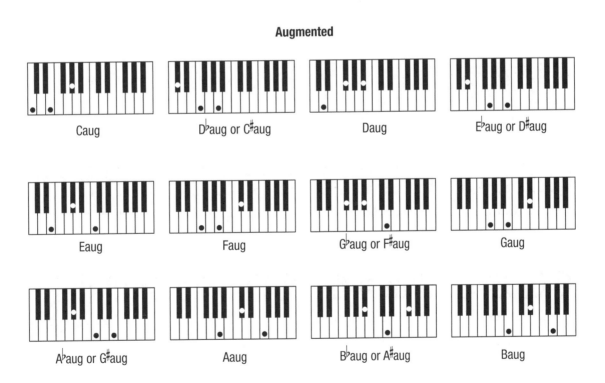

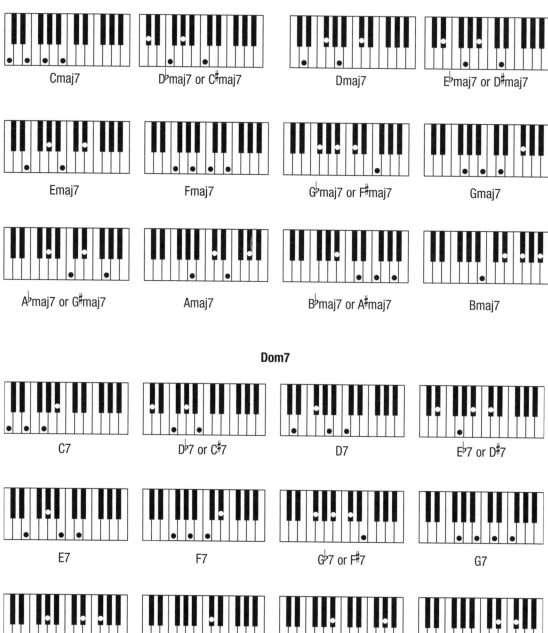

Minor7

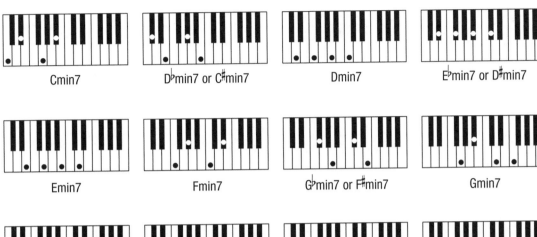

Cmin7 · D♭min7 or C#min7 · Dmin7 · E♭min7 or D#min7

Emin7 · Fmin7 · G♭min7 or F#min7 · Gmin7

A♭min7 or G#min7 · Amin7 · B♭min7 or A#min7 · Bmin7

Aug7

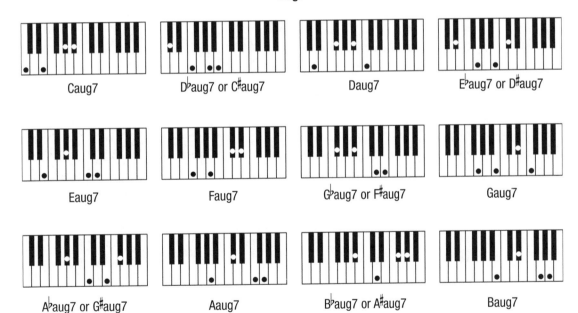

Caug7 · D♭aug7 or C#aug7 · Daug7 · E♭aug7 or D#aug7

Eaug7 · Faug7 · G♭aug7 or F#aug7 · Gaug7

A♭aug7 or G#aug7 · Aaug7 · B♭aug7 or A#aug7 · Baug7

Major6

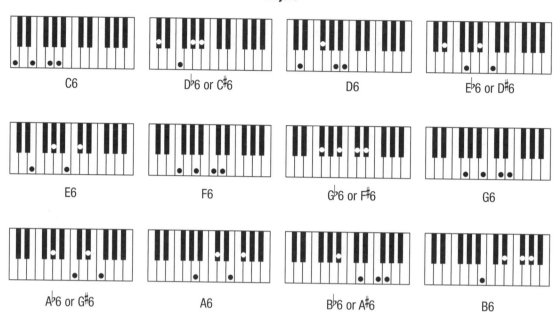

Minor6

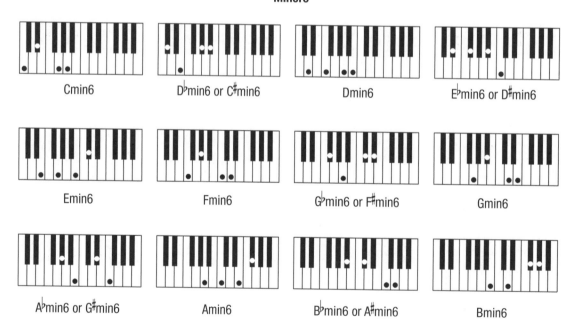

dim7

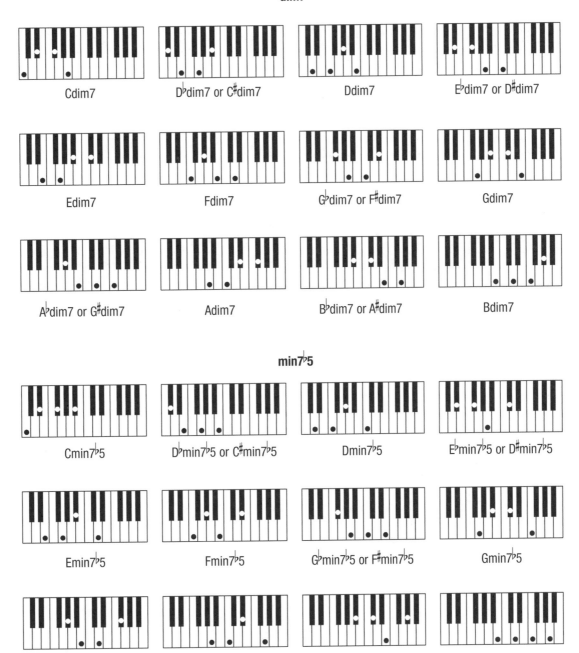

Cdim7

D♭dim7 or C♯dim7

Ddim7

E♭dim7 or D♯dim7

Edim7

Fdim7

G♭dim7 or F♯dim7

Gdim7

A♭dim7 or G♯dim7

Adim7

B♭dim7 or A♯dim7

Bdim7

min7♭5

Cmin7♭5

D♭min7♭5 or C♯min7♭5

Dmin7♭5

E♭min7♭5 or D♯min7♭5

Emin7♭5

Fmin7♭5

G♭min7♭5 or F♯min7♭5

Gmin7♭5

A♭min7♭5 or G♯min7♭5

Amin7♭5

B♭min7♭5 or A♯min7♭5

Bmin7♭5

7sus

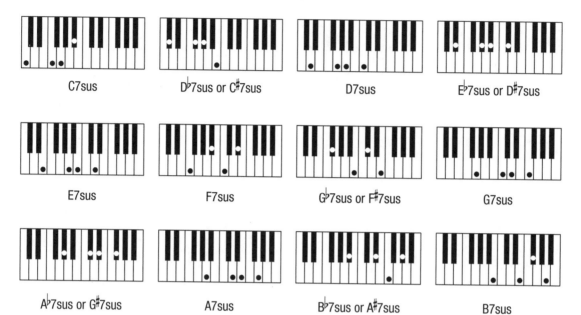

C7sus   D♭7sus or C♯7sus   D7sus   E♭7sus or D♯7sus

E7sus   F7sus   G♭7sus or F♯7sus   G7sus

A♭7sus or G♯7sus   A7sus   B♭7sus or A♯7sus   B7sus

Appendix C: Counting

Below are some of the more commonly seen note and rest values in music as applied to the 4/4 time signature.

Whole Note and Rest
Notice this note has no stem and is hollow. It will receive 4 beats. Notice how the rest hangs from the fourth line.

Half Note and Rest
This note is hollow and has a stem attached. It will receive 2 beats. Notice how the half rest sits on the third line.

Quarter Note and Rest
This note is solid and has a stem. It receives 1 beat. Notice how the quarter rest is a squiggly symbol that appears in place of a note.

Dotted Half Note
This note looks like the half note with a dot to the right of it. It will receive 3 beats. A dot (•) adds half the value of the note to its value.

Eighth Note and Rest
Notice how this note connects to other eighth notes with a bar at the top of the stem. Notice that the eighth note alone has a flag off the stem, as does the eighth rest. These notes receive $\frac{1}{2}$ beat each.

Dotted Quarter Note and Rest
Like on the dotted half note, the dot will add half of the note's value to it, making it $1\frac{1}{2}$ beats. Notice, too, how the dotted quarter rest will appear.

Triplet
These notes will appear like eighth notes, but have a numeral 3 over the 3-note grouping. These notes get a third of a beat each.

Sixteenths and Rests
These notes have 2 flags when they stand alone and two bars when they are connected to others. They receive a fourth of a beat. Observe how the rest looks, like the eighth-note rest but with 2 flags.

Appendix D: Scales

PRACTICING MAJOR SCALES

Major scales serve as an important fundamental skill that influences many areas of piano playing. Students practicing scales can improve their technique, their chord playing, and their improvisation skills.

Technique
Repetitive practice of scales gives you the ability to evenly play a steady series of notes. Finger control is learned as your fingers cross under and over with each scale. Speed becomes greater and more controlled in time. While playing scales, it is important to maintain correct finger placement.

The first 5 major scales, CGDAE, all have the same fingering. The following 7 scales have different fingerings, but notice that the thumbs (the pivot points) of both hands line up in each of these scales.

Chord Association
Scale parts, referred to as degrees, help you view the individual notes used in building chords. From left to right, the degrees of a scale are root, 2, 3, 4, 5, 6, 7, and 8, or octave. If you continue the scale beyond the octave, the degrees are 9, 10, 11, and so on. In the following pages, you will see how these degrees are used in building chords.

Improvisation
Scales often play an important part in the world of improvisation. Scales can be played using various sequences, shapes, and rhythms chosen from the available scale notes.

Appendix E: Building Your Own Chords

When you know your scales, you can make any chord yourself. It's easy.

The first concept to understand is that the degrees of a scale are numbered left to right from 1 to 7. In the next octave of the chord, the degrees run from 8 to 13.

After you have the numbering figured out, you create your chords by using these degrees from the scale. Here are the chords that you will see the most:

maj   1, 3, 5
min   1, ♭3, 5
dim   1, ♭3, ♭5
aug   1, 3, ♯5
maj7   1, 3, 5, 7
dom7   1, 3, 5, ♭7
min7   1, ♭3, 5, ♭7
min7♭5 1, ♭3, ♭5, ♭7
aug7   1, 3, ♯5, ♭7
7sus4   1, 4, 5, ♭7
dim7   1, ♭3, ♭5, ♭♭7
maj6   1, 3, 5, 6
min6   1, ♭3, 5, 6

There are endless variations on these chords that are created by adding, omitting, or altering various degrees of the scale. An example that occurs frequently is the min7♭5, shown above, which is a min7 with the 5 being flat. You could see Cmaj7♭5, Cmaj7♯5, Cmaj9, Cmin (maj7), and so forth. You won't often run across them. If you do, you can just play what you know that comes closest, or you can figure it out and pencil it in the piece.

Now you won't be stumped when you run across something that you have never seen before. Recently, one of my students came in with an Enya tune that had a Fadd9, so I showed her how to take a Fmaj and add the 9th to it. That's 1, 3, 5, 9 or F, A, C, G. It is that simple.

Inversions

Inversions are easy as well. What's an inversion? It's a chord fingering that doesn't start with the root of the chord as the bass note of the chord.

The 1st inversion starts with the 2nd note of the chord as the bass, and the 2nd inversion starts with the 3rd note of the chord as the bass.

Here's an example using a Cmaj:

Cmaj   C, E, G or 1, 3, 5
First Inversion: E, G, C or 3, 5, 8
Second Inversion: G, C, E or 5, 8, 10

Appendix F: Patterns—Endless Options

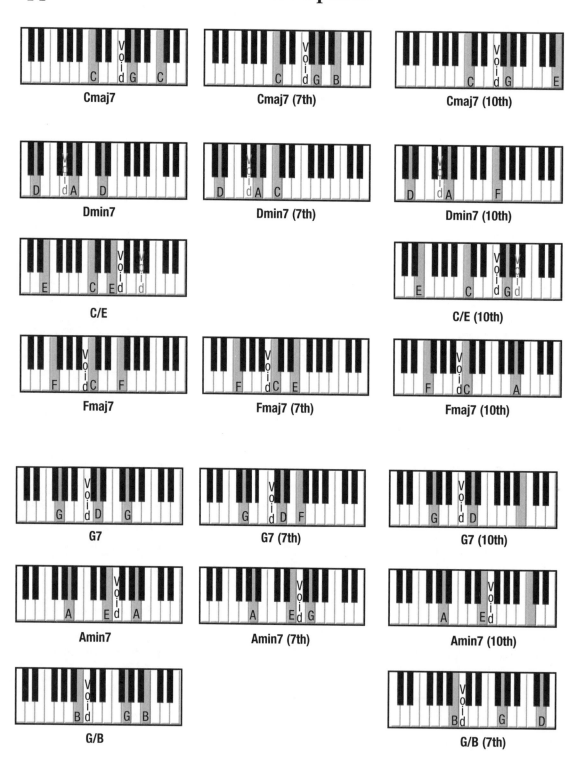

Cmaj7   Cmaj7 (7th)   Cmaj7 (10th)

Dmin7   Dmin7 (7th)   Dmin7 (10th)

C/E   C/E (10th)

Fmaj7   Fmaj7 (7th)   Fmaj7 (10th)

G7   G7 (7th)   G7 (10th)

Amin7   Amin7 (7th)   Amin7 (10th)

G/B   G/B (7th)

In this book, I introduce 3-note chordal patterns, which include the root, 5th, and 7th. There are endless pattern options that can be applied to melodies, and they are influenced by the style and rhythm of each piece of music. Listed below are a few of the many options you can choose while using chordal patterns. Don't be afraid to invent your own.

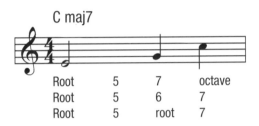

C maj7

Root	5	7	octave
Root	5	6	7
Root	5	root	7

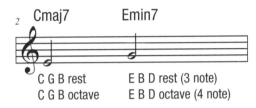

Cmaj7   Emin7

C G B rest   E B D rest (3 note)
C G B octave   E B D octave (4 note)

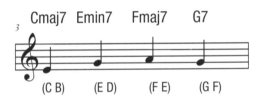

Cmaj7   Emin7   Fmaj7   G7

(C B)   (E D)   (F E)   (G F)

4-Note Patterns

You may extend the typical 3-note pattern into a 4-note structure. In $\frac{4}{4}$ time, this will keep the beats perfectly lined up. We are familiar with the root, 5th, 7th, and 6th, which can be organized in any formation you wish. For example, the root, 5, 7, octave may be played root, octave, 7, 5, etc.

8th-Note Patterns

Eighth-note patterns are common when you desire more movement in the Left Hand. They can be applied while using 3- or 4-note structure. Variations of these creations can be created. At times you may also *mix* the eighth- and quarter-note patterns within a piece of music.

Multiple Chord Bars

Often you will find multiple chords within a bar where applying pattern formations becomes nearly impossible. The first option would be to use only the *shell* (held or broken), or you may very well choose to remain active in the Left Hand by creating an eighth-note movement 1+2+3+4+. Each chord here will receive any 2-note combination chosen from a shell note or a pattern choice.

Various Time Signatures

Time signatures play an important part in the effect of just how many notes can fit within a bar. $\frac{3}{4}$ will clearly be able to fit a 3-note pattern. When the time signature moves to something not very common (like our $\frac{5}{4}$ example), you should view how many beats you have for each chord, and choose a pattern from the chord to fit. To extend your time using patterns, you can add another pulse within the pattern, giving the chord 5 beats or whatever you need.

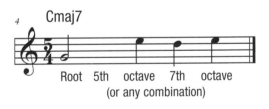

Cmaj7

Root 5th octave 7th octave
(or any combination)

Eighth notes can be used as well as creating a 10-note Left-Hand formation.

Improvising with these patterns is a very easy concept, yet difficult to master. The easy part is that you don't have to read the music; you just make it up as you go, and can't really be wrong. The hard part is that you have the freedom of endless choices and it is sometimes difficult to make choices. Here are some tips to get you started. Try them out and see what sounds good to you. Note that most tunes are created with a small number of repeating chord sequences or progressions.

Start out with a bar of Cmaj7 followed by a bar of Dmin7 and then back to a bar of Cmaj7.

Then try the progression Cmaj7, C/E, and Cmaj7.

Then try the progression Cmaj7, Fmaj7, Cmaj7
Cmaj7, G7, Cmaj7
Cmaj7, Amin7, Cmaj7
Cmaj7, B/G, Cmaj7

Then run through progressions starting with Dmin7, C/E, Fmaj7, etc.

See what sounds good to you.

You can expand to 4 chord progressions.

	Then:
Cmaj7, Dmin7, Fmaj7, Cmaj7	Cmaj7, C/E, Fmaj7, Cmaj7
Cmaj7, Dmin7, G7, Cmaj7	Cmaj7, C/E, G7, Cmaj7
Cmaj7, Dmin7, Amin7, Cmaj7	Cmaj7, C/E, Amin7, Cmaj7
Cmaj7, Dmin7, G/B, Cmaj7	Cmaj7, C/E, G/B, Cmaj7
	Cmaj7, C/E, Dim7, Cmaj7

As you run through these, you will run across progressions that sound good to you today. Play around with them to see where they might take you. An example of a progression that is used over and over is Cmaj7, Fmaj7, G7, and Cmaj7. You will find that many rock tunes and pop ballads use this progression.

As you get better and better with your play, you will find that you want to start creating patterns with other chords. I have designed this set of chords as an easy starting point; these are all white key chords that allow you to play in the key of C (all white keys). As you progress, you will want to create patterns for other chords and keys. You will be merging your knowledge of patterns and shells, leading you to the many options discussed at the end of Week 5.

Appendix G: Road Maps

 End of a section of the song.

 End of the song.

 Repeat signs: Repeat the music between the two signs.

 **Endings:** Play ending 1 the 1st time through, play ending 2 the 2nd time through, etc.

Fine **Fine:** A symbol to mark the end of the music.

 Coda: A symbol marking the "ending" or "tail" of a melody.

 Dal Segno: A symbol that means "from the sign."

D.C. al Fine: Da Capo al Fine "from the beginning to the end"; go back to the beginning of the song and repeat to the word *Fine*.

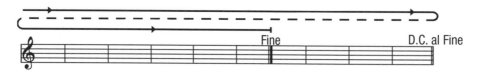

D.S. al Fine: Dal Segno al Fine "from the sign to the end"; go back to the Segno sign and repeat to the word *Fine*.

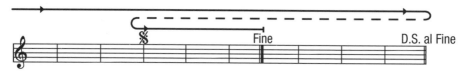

D.C. al Coda:

Da Capo al Coda "from the beginning to the ending"; go back to the beginning of the song, play to the coda sign; and skip to the coda at the end of the song.

D.S. al Coda: Dal Segno al Coda "from the sign to the ending"; go back to the segno sign, play to the coda sign; and skip to the coda at the end of the song.

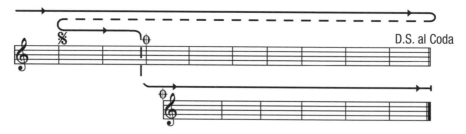

Appendix H: 3rds

This is the final component to basic chord structure.

C Scale · **3rd**

Not a Traditional Triad Approach

I choose to present the 3rd as an individual element that can be used in the Right Hand, and not as part of a memorized triad. The 3rd of a chord is one of the most important components of a chord's structure. It is also one of the more difficult tones to learn. Unlike the 7ths, where we use a simple formula of 1, 2, 3 notes down from the octave, the 3rd tone is best put to memory using visual tricks that work for you. Unlike a traditional approach of learning the 3rds amidst triad formations, I prefer to drop the 3rd into the Right Hand, adding to our strong foundation of the shell and the 5th. By breaking the 3rd away from a grouped learning of triads, you will become much more in control of this note and be able to use it in other situations. This process places emphasis on *2-handed* chordal structures, which ultimately are what professional pianists love to control, because the chord will sound between 2 hands, and not just under 1.

Teaching the 3rds is beyond the scope of this book. If you want to try inserting some 3rds in your playing, find the 3rds from your knowledge of scales or by looking at the chords in Appendix B and extracting the 3rds.

3rd or ♭3rd

The 3rd will always be getting adjusted to conform to a wide selection of chord structures. The 3rd will be flat on all minor and diminished chords, including minor7, minor7♭5, diminished7, and minor6, lending itself to a (minor tonality) darker sound. Keep the 3rd natural on all major, dominant, and augmented chords.

On Compression

As shown in the first illustration, the 3rd of the Cmaj7 is the E and is placed below the melody note into the right hand. It is played *on* the compression. This is more difficult than the tonal movement option outlined below, because you have to place down 4 notes at the same time.

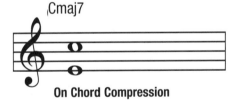

Cmaj7

On Chord Compression

Tonal Movement

As shown in the second illustration, the 3rd may be placed in as a delayed sound, or what I refer to as a *tonal movement*. This adds great interest and can be used in conjunction with other tones dropped in as tonal movements.

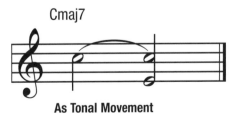

Cmaj7

As Tonal Movement

Left-Hand Patterns and 3rds

The 3rd may be added into the Left-Hand-Pattern formations. One example: 1, 7, 3 or 1, 7, 10 (which is the 3rd above the octave). Endless Left-Hand-Pattern options can be formed as the 3rd becomes the new added option amidst your note selections.

Appendix I: Reading Exercises

Index

About the Authors

Dan Delaney

Dan is a professional pianist, college educator/lecturer, and well-known author and videographer. Over the last two decades, Dan has produced a variety of forms of instructional media for all levels of piano playing. From his instructional video correspondence to CD-ROM courses, Dan uses his creativity to bring cutting-edge instruction into the home.

Dan attended the Berklee School of Music in Boston, where he began gaining recognition as a performer while learning the ins-and-outs of the business. Now with thirty years of experience behind him, he has polished his teaching skills with his revolutionary video correspondence course, multimedia software courses, and internet piano instruction courses. He reaches all levels of students in all four corners of the world. You can find his students playing on hit Broadway shows, in jazz clubs, on cruise ships, in their homes, and at school recitals. He currently teaches at two colleges, teaches privately, teaches via the internet, is the house pianist at the Ritz Carlton Phoenix, and performs regularly with his jazz trio.

Bill Chotkowski

Bill Chotkowski is a graduate of the Massachusetts Institute of Technology and has spent his career making computers easy to use for ordinary people. He is one of those inventive people who have shaped how computers are used today. From digital imaging to icons on your desktop, Bill has been instrumental in the development of the things you use everyday on your PC. For example, PC users have benefited from his creativity: The original tan briefcase icon that appears on the Windows desktop was drawn from Bill's own leather Coach briefcase in 1989 (possibly the most pictured briefcase in the world).

Recently, Bill has been electronically publishing personal instruction titles with the same level of fun and ingenuity that he has brought to computers. He understands what it takes to present information in an enjoyable, yet concise, format and knows how to lead a reader through the coursework while reaching their goals every step of the way.